Living the Life You Always Wanted

Experience Peace, Joy, Power,

and Perfect Love

in Times of Uncertainty

Living the Life You Always Wanted

Experience Peace, Joy, Power, and Perfect Love in Times of Uncertainty

Debby Sibert

2020 by Debby Sibert
All Rights Reserved
Printed in the United States of America

ISBN: 978-1-7354159-2-5

Published by Ultimately Essential, Oak Hill, VA

Unless otherwise noted, all Scripture is from the Holy Bible, English Standard Version. ESV® Text Edition: 2016. Copyright © 2001 by Crossway Bibles, a publishing ministry of Good News Publishers.

Scripture quotations marked NLT are taken from the *Holy Bible*, New Living Translation, copyright © 1996, 2004, 2015 by Tyndale House Foundation. Used by permission of Tyndale House Publishers, Inc., Carol Stream, Illinois 60188. All rights reserved.

Scripture marked KJV are from the King James Version, Public Domain

Scripture marked NIV are from THE HOLY BIBLE, NEW INTERNATIONAL VERSION®, NIV® Copyright © 1973, 1978, 1984, 2011 by Biblica, Inc.® Used by permission. All rights reserved worldwide.

The words from the Hymn, "It is Well with My Soul" by Horatio Spafford has been taken from the Public Domain.

A Note from the Author:

It is my passion to help people discover their life's purpose while empowering them to unlock their God-given potential.

It is my heart's desire that everyone would have an opportunity to meet Jesus—to experience Him intimately, to have their hearts transformed by His love and grace, and to learn the peace, joy, and victory that comes from a "sold-out" life of surrender and obedience. Are you "All In" for Christ?

A Note from my Pastor:

"I am so thankful for Debby Sibert – for her writing, for her teaching, and for her life! She is the real deal. She loves God's Word, and she loves helping people experience abundant life according to God's good design. You will be blessed, encouraged, challenged, and ultimately changed by God's grace through her."

David Platt, New York Times Best Selling Author
Lead Pastor, McLean Bible Church

Acknowledgments

To my wonderful husband, who has sacrificed many days and nights of solitude while I worked tirelessly on this manuscript, thank you also for your prayers, for proofreading, editing, and providing your valuable feedback along the way. God has used you mightily to help me become the wife, mother, friend, and Christ-follower I am today. You inspire me with your life of honesty, integrity, and servant leadership, as well as your love and devotion. This just scratches the surface of your many qualities I hope have rubbed off on me over these forty years of sharing life together. You are my rock. Thank you for believing in me and supporting me to fulfill God's purpose in finally getting this book out of my head and heart and into print.

I also thank my many friends—you know who you are, who have cheered me on and given me your feedback along the way. Your input, friendship, and love have been priceless, and I appreciate it so much!

To my pastor of almost thirty years, Lon Solomon, who unknowingly consistently mentored me from the pulpit, inspiring me to speak the truth about the gospel boldly, I thank you. My current pastor, David Platt, I thank you for the continuing challenge to deepen my faith and live it out daily with a mission mindset. Both of you have contributed greatly to my understanding of the importance of total surrender and obedience.

Most of all, I thank God not only for saving me for eternity but for how He continues to pursue me and teach me what it looks like to be fully surrendered to Him. What a ride! I am a slow learner, so I constantly thank Him for His patience with me. I thank Him for not giving up on me and for chasing after me until I relented to write this book as well as the others He has commissioned me to get out of my head and heart and into print. I pray the contents of this book will take your life to the next level as it has mine.

Table of Contents

Introduction 1
Chapter 1 - What Happens When We Receive Christ as Our Savior? 13
    Transformation requires Spiritual Training 17
    Let's Talk About Freedom... 22
    Diving Deeper... 31
Chapter 2 - Can We Lose Our Salvation? 33
    Diving Deeper... 41
Chapter 3 - Obstacles to Grace... 43
    Diving Deeper... 55
Chapter 4 - What Is the Victorious Life and How Do We Live It?...... 57
    What is Victory in the Life of a Christian? 58
    How Does Christ Come to Live Inside Us as the Holy Spirit?......... 62
    Perfect Love - What Is it and How Do We Live It?........... 64
    Suttender - What is it, and What Do We Need to Do?...... 72
    Diving Deeper... 77
Chapter 5 - What Does Total Surrender Look Like?................. 79
    Diving Deeper... 93
Chapter 6 - The Impact of Forgiveness..................................... 95
    What is forgiveness? 96
    My Story.. 100
    Diving Deeper... 107
Chapter 7 - The Victorious Life Is a Gift 109
    So, What is Obedience?.. 112
    Diving Deeper... 119

- Chapter 8 - Still Feel like You're Struggling with Known Sin? 121
  - Diving Deeper 127
- Chapter 9 - How Does Suffering Fit in With a Victorious Life? 129
  - How Do We Respond to Suffering? 133
  - Diving Deeper 145
- Chapter 10 - What Are You Afraid Of? 147
  - What Is Fear? 148
  - What Is Depression? 150
  - What Is Anxiety? 154
  - What Is God's Agenda for Us? 160
  - How Should We Deal With Fear and Anxiety? 162
  - What I Learned about Fear 164
  - Are You Fearful of Your Future? 165
  - Diving Deeper 167
- Chapter 11 - Life Lessons Learned From a Shepherd 169
  - There Can be no Christianity Without the Cross 179
  - Diving Deeper 181
- Chapter 12 - The Impact of Prayer 183
  - General Thoughts on The Purpose and Importance of Prayer 189
  - Diving Deeper 195
- Chapter 13 - Practical Application 197
  - Daily Disciplines to Experience the Victorious Life 198
  - Diving Deeper 203
- Chapter 14 - Best Practices Going Forward 205
  - Next Steps to Take Your Life to the Next Level 205
  - Diving Deeper 221
- Epilogue 223

Do You Want Debby's *FREE* Follow-Up Book?	227
Appendix - Attributes of God	229
Resources - Recommended Reading:	237
Notes	239

INTRODUCTION

I recently heard a story about a father walking with his son, and his little boy asked him, "Daddy, how big is God?"

His father pointed up to the sky and asked, "How big is that airplane?"

The little boy said, "It's so small I can hardly see it.

Then the father took his son to the airport, and as they approached a plane, he asked him, "How big is the airplane now?"

The little boy said, "Oh my goodness, it's huge!"

The father said, "God is like that too, son. The size of God depends on how close or far you are to Him. The closer you are, the greater He will be in your life!"

May I just add that if you have big problems, maybe your god is too small. If you have a big God, you will find your problems are very small.

Does the life you are experiencing right now line up with what you know God offers through the Scriptures? Do you ever feel lethargic and distant from God? If you were to die today, would most people assume you were going to heaven as they look at your lifestyle? What you seek is what you get. What are you seeking? Do you lack peace or joy in your life—feeling stuck in your Christian walk? Do you find yourself wondering if there is more to the "abundant, victorious" life?

If you have big problems, maybe your god is too small. If you have a big God, you will find your problems are very small.

1

Too often, we settle for far less than what God wants to do in and through us. Do you sense there may be more God wants to do in and through you than you are currently experiencing? Do you want to take your life experience to the next level? If your answer is "yes" to any of these questions, then this book is for you.

Are you shaped by the world or by the Word of God? Have you bought into the lie that the world and all it offers will bring you peace, joy, power, or perfect love? If you're going to experience God's best, you have to trust Him to give you what you need to get through life. How do you get to experience the victorious life? That's the question this book answers.

As a Christ-follower, we are "more than conquerors through Christ" according to the Scriptures. We can and should be "overcomers," however, many are not experiencing the joy or victory in Christ that is possible. I wish someone had shared with me the concepts, truths, and tips in this book early in my Christian walk. It would have saved me a lot of time wandering in the spiritual desert of isolation I experienced early on.

Let me tell you a story I found on Randy Alcorn's blog to see if you resonate with the truth of it. I want to make sure we are on the same page so you can know you are ready to proceed with the encouragement and process of living an abundant, empowered life. I told this story in a previous book I wrote, but I think it is worth repeating because it's a great story. I hope to inspire you to soar beyond your current horizons. I have a crucial question for you. Have you made your reservation yet for heaven, and are you sure your name is written in the Lamb's Book of Life?

Ruthanna Metzgar, a professional singer, tells a story that illustrates the importance of having our names written in "The Book." Several years ago, she was asked to sing at the wedding of a very wealthy man.

Introduction

According to the invitation, the reception would be held on the top two floors of Seattle's Columbia Tower, the Northwest's tallest skyscraper. She and her husband, Roy, were excited about attending.

At the reception, waiters in tuxedos offered luscious hors d'oeuvres and exotic beverages. The bride and groom approached a beautiful glass and brass staircase that led to the top floor. Someone ceremoniously cut a satin ribbon draped across the bottom of the stairs. They announced the wedding feast was about to begin. Bride and groom ascended the stairs, followed by their guests.

At the top of the stairs, a maître d' with a bound book greeted the guests outside the doors.

"May I have your name, please?"

"I am Ruthanna Metzgar, and this is my husband, Roy."

He searched the M's.

"I'm not finding it. Would you spell it, please?"

Ruthanna spelled her name slowly. After searching the book, the maître d' looked up and said, "I'm sorry, but your name isn't here."

"There must be some mistake," Ruthanna replied. "I'm the singer. I sang for this wedding!"

The gentleman answered, "It doesn't matter who you are or what you did. Without your name in the book, you cannot attend the banquet."

He motioned to a waiter and said, "Show these people to the service elevator, please."

The Metzgars followed the waiter past beautifully decorated tables laden with shrimp, whole smoked salmon, and magnificent carved ice sculptures. Adjacent to the banquet area, an orchestra was preparing to perform, the musicians all dressed in dazzling white tuxedos.

The waiter led Ruthanna and Roy to the service elevator, ushered them in, and pushed G for the parking garage.

After locating their car and driving several miles in silence, Roy reached over and put his hand on Ruthanna's arm. "Sweetheart, what happened?"

"When the invitation arrived, I was busy," Ruthanna replied. "I never bothered to RSVP. Besides, I was the singer. Surely I could go to the reception without returning the RSVP!"

Ruthanna started to weep—not only because she had missed the most lavish banquet she'd ever been invited to, but also because she suddenly had a small taste of what it will be like someday for people as they stand before Christ and find their names are not written in the Lamb's Book of Life.

Throughout the ages, countless people have been too busy to respond to Christ's invitation to his wedding banquet. Many assume that the good they've done—perhaps attending church, being baptized, singing in the choir, or helping in a soup kitchen—will be enough to gain entry to heaven. But people who do not respond to Christ's invitation to forgive their sins are people whose names aren't written in the Lamb's Book of Life. To be denied entrance to heaven's wedding banquet will not just mean going down the service elevator to the garage. It will mean being cast outside into Hell forever.

On that day, no explanation or excuse will count. All that will matter is whether our names are written in the book. If they're not, we'll be turned away.

Introduction

Have you said yes to Christ's invitation to join him at the wedding feast and spend eternity with Him in His house? If so, you have reason to rejoice—Heaven's gates will be open to you.

If you have been putting off your response, your RSVP, or if you presume that you can enter heaven without responding to Christ's invitation, one day you will deeply regret it.[1]

This is a rather sobering thought, isn't it? Over many years of leading or co-leading Christian groups of various sizes with people of diverse backgrounds in and outside the church environment, I am saddened by how few individuals have even thought about where they might spend eternity. Do you know how long that is? Most people I talk to seem to fixate on just enjoying the "here and now" with little thought about the future, so they probably have no assurance of heaven.

Even among the Christians I've met, so many are not enjoying the benefits and joy of surrender and obedience, leading to an empowered, victorious life. Their day-to-day existence doesn't reveal the power and joy that should reflect a transformed life.

Barna does extensive research, polling American professing Christians, and found some interesting statistics. Of those he polled in 2011, 78% stated they agreed that spirituality is very important to them, and yet only 18% claimed to be "completely dependent on God." That helps to explain why 52% believe there is much more to the Christian life than what they have experienced. Only 12% recognized the significance of their sins causing them to experience this relationship gap, and only 3% of those self-identified American Christians polled indicated that they have surrendered control of their life to God, submitted to His will for their life, and devoted themselves to loving and serving God and others.[2]

Now maybe you can see why I have felt so compelled to write this book. I *know* there are many Christians missing out on experiencing the fullness of intimacy with Christ simply because they do not realize how much more there is to discover or how far they have drifted. If this is you, I encourage you to read on!

The longer we drift, the harder it is to come back to the lordship of Christ. Remember, God's faithfulness in the past provides perspective for your future. If you feel like you're drifting away from God, you're probably not being proactive in your pursuit of seeking Him. For me, this has been a long journey. Like everyone else, I have had my share of ups and downs, but I have learned so much over all these years of walking with Christ, and I long to share with you my failures, victories, revelations, and experiences.

The world is swift to tell us how we are lacking and what it offers is contrary to the teachings of the Word of God. Too often, those voices drown out the still, small voice of God, which ultimately has all the answers that lead to a victorious life—the life you always wanted. So few seem to hear it or even understand how important it is to know God and how to have a close relationship with Him.

For the past sixteen years, my husband, Bob, and I have been mentoring couples struggling in their marriages. We meet regularly with them, walking alongside them, giving biblical advice and counsel. We also have been on panels, facilitated many marriage courses, conferences, and seminars. Currently, we are also working with small groups of couples wanting to take their marriages to the next level. It was a result of many of these interactions that prompted me to write this book.

Over all these years of working with couples from all kinds of backgrounds, we have found many are missing the mark because their relationship with God is not where it should be. Either they don't have a

Introduction

relationship with Christ at all, or they have let their focus be inward, looking to have the world revolve around them, fulfilling their desires and wishes. As a result, they have missed the purpose God has for them. We are all born as selfish sinners, and marriage has a way of showing us through our spouse (much like a mirror) just how flawed we are. Surrendering to God, looking out for the best interest of our spouse, and being a servant lover just doesn't come naturally.

I know many Christians (married or not) are living defeated lives and not experiencing the victorious life available to them—the life they expected to experience as a Christ-follower. There are many reasons for this, which this book addresses. Still, my primary purpose and focus are to hopefully inspire *you* to realize what might be missing in your walk with the Lord and share how you can experience the amazing relationship that is possible. I would love to help you get on track to experiencing all the Lord wants for you so you can experience the life you always wanted. If you feel like you are often missing the joy, peace, and power of God in your life, read on!

My intention in writing this book is to encourage anyone wanting to take their spiritual life to the next level. The cornerstone of the extraordinarily victorious, transformed Christian life is a vital spiritual union with the risen Christ—available only through God's grace. When God created you, He created a masterpiece, and He has an exceptional plan and purpose for your life. If you are not sure what that is, I hope to help you figure it out with the use of Scripture, referring to our "Life's Manual" (the Bible) as the foundation of that discovery.

I also had considered this could be a great resource to use in a small group study. I included questions at the end of every chapter for discussion and application to reflect on and challenge each of us. I call it "Diving Deeper."

We must act on what we know Scripture requires of us. To read God's commands and ignore them is such a waste. God wants so much more for you. Reading God's Word is like holding up a mirror in which we can see our faces—our character, values, etc. It gives us a perspective of our life and relationships we can't see on our own. It also opens up a window in which we can see Christ looking back at us. When we compare our image to that of Christ, we can see how we are doing—the similarities, the differences, and perhaps where we need to concentrate our efforts to improve.

One miraculous claim of the Bible is it *is* possible by gazing consistently into that mirror and acting on the Holy Spirit's guidance, that God can truly change us from the inside out, resulting in a kind of metamorphosis. I know He has changed my life. It's indeed possible to grow to be more like Christ at a heart level than we are today. A transformed life is possible because, as a Christ-follower, Christ lives inside us in the person of the Holy Spirit. We will be talking about how this life is a journey, but we must take that first step.

Traumatic events can cause a life to shatter, but few people grow or experience transformation dramatically during adulthood. Personal growth or even consistent growth is rare. When it *does* happen, it's usually because something miraculously occurred in their life. It's only the Spirit of God, through the Word of God, often with the help of the people of God that can produce such an extraordinary transformation in someone open to change.

> *A transformed life is possible because, as a Christ-follower, Christ lives inside us in the person of the Holy Spirit.*

Sadly, many Bible study groups settle for education *about* God and the Christian life rather than the *application* of how we can become like

INTRODUCTION

Christ. Many don't believe it's possible. Some like the idea in theory, but the process of change frightens them. Many don't seem to want to give up their well-worn paths to strike out on the uncharted seas of God's ways. There is a fear that letting go of the familiar will allow the Spirit to break up their cemented habits like a jackhammer. Hopefully, those in your group or your accountability partners are committed to becoming Christ-like. That way, you can help each other to be, look, and act more like Christ.

Very likely, though, your group may contain some decent people who "sort of" want to follow Christ but aren't that eager to see their lives disturbed. All of us are busy with responsibilities, jobs, families, bills, and chores. With such duties, there just doesn't seem to be enough hours also to contemplate the face of Christ and the condition of one's heart. As long as things are going well, we don't feel the need to do so.

I hope the content of this book and my discussion questions will challenge and invite you to apply the Word of God in your life. As a result of this, I hope you'll see the realities of the human condition, ways to allow a transformation in your heart to focus on God's purpose for your life, and how God might use you to encourage others.

I have been blessed to be under incredible teaching, discipling, and Bible study most of my adult life and have learned and experienced so much. This is how God prepared me to get me through some life-altering experiences I've had and will be sharing with you in these pages. I can't wait to share some of the lessons I've learned along the way.

Especially if you feel like you are in a spiritual rut, this book is for you. You can experience an abundant, victorious life of transformation no matter what storms, valleys, or mountains you might encounter. It's important to know that even though you may feel like you are experiencing a tsunami in your life right now, if it were not for storms, there would be no rainbows. You *can* have incredible peace that passes all understanding (See Philippians 4:7). Life is a journey, and this book is your roadmap to victory. Your mission, should you choose to accept it, is to learn how to experience the life you always wanted—an extraordinary, victorious, transformed life.

Transformation does not come from trying hard, but from believing the truth. It comes from spiritual training. I think many Christians want to change and rid themselves of some bad habits and maybe even some issues of bondage but don't understand the impact of spiritual training that can produce transformation.

> *Transformation does not come from trying hard, but from believing the truth.*

God wants you to not just gain intellectual knowledge of His truth, but also to experience it. With God's help and the guidance provided in this book, you can do this! You can experience the peace, joy, power, and perfect love that only a life surrendered to God can have. Some things about Jesus, you can only learn as you obey Him, and we cannot really *know* Him unless we *experience* Him. Your obedience will lead you to a greater understanding of who He is, and your eyes will be opened to how you can best serve Him. I praise God that you responded to His pursuit of you to pick up this book to help you get the clarity you need to "fill in the gaps" for you.

If you are a Christ-follower, God has chosen you—what a blessing! I would like to quote a couple different sections of Scripture by Paul in the New Testament. They present kind of a challenge, but somewhat encapsulate where I hope we end up and accomplish, using God's tools, by the end of this book. They are a summary of Christian virtues which provide the foundational principles of a healthy spiritual life and the priorities for successful Christian living:

Introduction

- Put on then, as God's chosen ones, holy and beloved, compassionate hearts, kindness, humility, meekness, and patience, bearing with one another and, if one has a complaint against another, forgiving each other; as the Lord has forgiven you, so you also must forgive. And above all these put on love, which binds everything together in perfect harmony. And let the peace of Christ rule in your hearts, to which indeed you were called in one body. And be thankful. Let the word of Christ dwell in you richly, teaching and admonishing one another in all wisdom, singing psalms and hymns and spiritual songs, with thankfulness in your hearts to God. And whatever you do, in word or deed, do everything in the name of the Lord Jesus, giving thanks to God the Father through him (Colossians 3:12-17).

- Rejoice always, pray without ceasing, give thanks in all circumstances; for this is the will of God in Christ Jesus for you. Do not quench the Spirit. Do not despise prophecies, but test everything; hold fast what is good. Abstain from every form of evil (1 Thessalonians 5:16-22).

We cannot be like Christ without these attitudes and attributes. Our daily lives must exhibit who we already are in our relationship with Christ. You can do this, and this can be your life! You have the opportunity and what it takes to fulfill God's plan for your future. You can experience more in your life than you ever thought possible as long as you are "All In."

I write like I talk, and have written this book as if you and I are close friends (which I hope we are someday). I hope this gives me permission to be honest and straightforward—speaking the truth in love as I write. ☺

Paul, in many of his letters, challenged his readers to imitate him or to be imitators of Him. I know he strove to imitate Christ, so I have tried to take that challenge to heart. I've noticed he always starts his letters with a greeting extending grace and peace. He then would tell the recipients that he thanked God continually in his prayers for them, while encouraging them in their faith.

On that note, I would like to extend the same to you with the confidence that you have picked up this book with the desire to take your life to the next level with your Lord and Savior. My prayer for you as you read through this is that God will meet you where you are and take you to where He would love for you to be so that you can experience the most from and with Him. You *can* live the life you always wanted and experience peace, power, and erfect love in times of uncertainty

Chapter 1

What Happens When We Receive Christ as Our Savior?

Before we dig deep, let's review some foundational principles. This is a bit of a synopsis from my first book, *Where Will You Spend Eternity?* It's never a bad idea to examine the critical components of the Christian life to be sure we are on the same page.

When we become a Christ-follower, we literally *do* receive Him, in that His Spirit, the Holy Spirit, takes up residence in our hearts. Jesus *is* our life! Romans 8:9 says: "You, however, are not in the flesh but in the Spirit, if the Spirit of God dwells in you. Anyone who does not have the Spirit of Christ does not belong to him."

If you recall, when you asked Jesus to come into your life, according to 2 Corinthians 5:17, you became "...a new creation. The old has passed away; behold the new has come."

It doesn't say you are a new and improved version of your old self but a "new" creature with a *new* nature! Your spiritual DNA is different since you now have the "seed" of Christ living in you having been "born again" spiritually. This rebirth will result in you living fundamentally differently since you are "in Christ." We miraculously receive a heart transplant!

> *Your spiritual DNA is different since you now have the "seed" of Christ living in you having been "born again" spiritually. This rebirth will result in you living fundamentally differently since you are "in Christ."*

If you have not yet made that commitment, please pick up my first book. Then, come back and read this to learn how to take your new life to a whole new level. God wants all His children to experience the benefits of a surrendered life, letting Him live His perfect life of love and holiness in and through you. There is so much even many Christians are not experiencing because of their lack of proper focus and priorities. That is what we will unpack throughout these pages. God has so many blessings in store for you!

We are all a product of our past, but that no longer defines us. I don't know what you found your security in before, but when you find your identity in the One who created you, it changes your whole perspective on life. How awesome is that! With the confidence it gives you, knowing you are loved, valued, and significant, you no longer experience a need to impress anyone else. When we become a Christ-follower, our new identity is in Christ! We no longer belong to ourselves or anyone else. We are His!

> *When you find your identity in the One who created you, it changes your whole perspective on life.*

It is my prayer if you haven't already, that you fall in love with Jesus as I have. If you make Him the priority in your life and learn to make Him Lord as well as Savior, you will experience the abundant, empowered life. "When Christ becomes the first place in your heart, you will experience victory—the life you always wanted."

If you know Christ but find yourself living far from God, feeling defeated or "stuck," and just not growing or thriving in your walk with Him but want to, this book will help you deepen that relationship and experience the victorious Christian life. Only God's power can overcome our sinful nature and give us new life.

One reason you might be feeling stuck might be,

> When we are born of God, we get His nature, but He does not immediately take away all the old nature. Each species of animal and bird is true to its nature. You can tell the nature of the dove or canary bird. The stallion is true to his nature; the cow is true to hers. But we humans have two natures and do not let the world or Satan make you think that the old nature is extinct, because it is not.
>
> Though it is subdued, the old nature in the believer never dies; and unless we are watchful and prayerful, it will gain the upper hand, and rush us into sin. Someone has pointed out that "I" is the center of S-I-N. It is the medium through which Satan acts. And so the worst enemy you have to overcome, after all, is yourself.[1]

I know we all have been there. I can speak from experience, it can be quite a struggle, especially when, in our residual sinful nature, we take back control at times. That's the problem with being a "living" sacrifice. It means we'll get up on the altar of surrender, but then we keep crawling down when times get tough. ☺

I'm encouraged that even the apostle Paul struggled with this. He tells us in Romans 7 how he struggled with the kind of ever-present sin nature and the tension we all experience. Thankfully, despite all that, he discovered and recorded for us in Romans 8:1, "There is therefore now no condemnation for those who are in Christ Jesus."

The Holy Spirit, which comes to live inside us when we become followers of Christ, is much better at leading and guiding our lives than we ever could. Still, sometimes we tend to forget that and take back control, to our detriment.

Once we become serious about our walk with Christ, our life mission is to glorify God in and through our life. I will show you ways to do that throughout this book. Once you truly make this commitment, your life will change, and you will desire to do this. In Romans 12:2, Paul tells us: "Do not be conformed to this world, but be transformed by the renewal of your mind, that by testing you may discern what is the will of God, what is good and acceptable and perfect."

The process of transformation will only happen with our willful participation and action. Over time as your life transforms more and more in Christ's image, your life and countenance will radiate with His love, and you will draw others to Him.

Christ is invisible, but He lives in and through you. You are to be an extension of Him to the world exemplifying, through the power of the Holy Spirit, His life of unconditional love, humility, grace, and servanthood and to live out His character qualities of the fruit of the Spirit. Galatians 5:22–24 states: "But the fruit of the Spirit is love, joy, peace, patience, kindness, goodness, faithfulness, gentleness, self-control; against such things there is no law. And those who belong to Christ Jesus have crucified the flesh with its passions and desires."

When I became serious about my faith as a college student, I found these verses, and I clung to them as my life's goal, with God's help—to achieve these character qualities in my life—a goal that has served me well all these years. I challenge you to do the same.

If we allow our sinful attitudes to resurface continually, they will stifle the fruit of the Spirit in our lives and hurt our witness. For example, if you still struggle with a temper, you may prevent someone from coming to faith. Your overbearing ambition might influence you to use others to reach your goals, and your selfishness might hinder you from being a blessing to others—just to name a few. You really cannot get away with saying, "Well, that's just the way I am." Maybe you "were," but that person died with Christ. You are now a new creation.

As God's children, we should bear the indelible stamp of His moral character. We should be loving, gracious, and generous, even to the point of praying for those who persecute us (Matthew 5:44). That's a tall order, isn't it?

There was never a man who walked with more integrity than Jesus. In fact, He is the epitome of integrity we should emulate. This is the kind of change you can see taking place in your life. Don't be discouraged if you feel so far from achieving this. Remember, life is a journey.

LIVING OUT TRANSFORMATION REQUIRES SPIRITUAL TRAINING

Our spiritual training begins with personal integrity. There is no hope of transformation without it. God wants us to worship Him in spirit and truth, and unless we learn to be honest with ourselves, Him, and others, then change can never occur.

So what is "spiritual training?" It's digging into the Word of God, our life's manual to learn the ways and will of God. It is to study Jesus who came not only to save us but also to be the example of how we are to live our lives on this earth. It is to learn from His followers the impact He had on them and will have on us if we let Him change our heart to align with His.

Any athlete can tell you it takes much training to become proficient in any sport. No one can run a marathon if they aren't a runner who has built up their endurance, nor can someone climb Kilimanjaro without the proper training. A swimmer has to gradually increase their swimming distance before swimming the 2.4 miles required in an ironman race. Getting into shape is not about trying, but about training. The same is true in the Christian life.

No doubt about it, the Christian life is hard work. But with the proper spiritual training, Christianity teaches us how to systematically implement the truths of God's Word into our lives. Don't worry. As a Christ-follower, you have the power of the Holy Spirit in your life, which gives you the ability to do all things within God's will. He is your life coach. If we walk by the Spirit, then we will not gratify the desires of the flesh (Galatians 5:16).

It is my prayer that God will transform your heart through the gospel of Jesus Christ by the in-depth and continuous work of the Holy Spirit as you make Jesus the object of your affections. Transformation does not come from knowledge but from obedience to what we know.

> *Transformation does not come from knowledge but from obedience to what we know.*

The fact you have a relationship with God places immeasurable value on your life. The treasure of God's wisdom and knowledge is available to you through Christ as well as His perfect love. You now have access to peace that passes all understanding as well as compassion for others that is supernatural. When Jesus lives in you, everything available to Him also dwells in you.

Remember the same God who created the universe, the same Jesus who rose from the dead and the same Holy Spirit who inspired the writing of the Holy Scriptures (the Bible), which is the book we live by, actually lives in you! Through the power of the indwelling Holy Spirit—"Christ in you" (Romans 8:10-11), you have direct access to God and His infinite wisdom. How tremendous is that!

One heart change you should notice in yourself, especially if it is contrary to how you used to be, is an attitude of gratitude. When you are a follower of Christ, there is no reason *not* to be grateful, no matter what the circumstances, and that is something that does not come naturally. We have so much for which to be thankful. When we have Jesus, we not only have eternal life; we have so much more. *He* is all we need.

> *Our degree of thankfulness is a barometer of our soul.*

If we stop being thankful for what we do have, our focus can easily drift to what we don't have, leading to discontentment and an ungrateful heart. If we find ourselves in that state, we need to stop and ask ourselves, "Who's in charge." When Jesus is Lord, our heart overflows with gratitude because He calls the shots. Our degree of thankfulness is a barometer of our soul.

Did you know your brain cannot be disgruntled and grateful at the same time? So you have to choose what kind of attitude you want to have from now on. When we live in light of eternity, our values change, don't they? Jesus gives us everything we need to live for Him. Life is full of choices, and the more serious you become about your faith journey, you will find yourself making much better choices.

We all have a natural tendency to bring some baggage into our adult lives. It's not easy to shake behaviors and attitudes that were modeled to us and been our "norm" while growing up. You may have had stellar role models and seen Christ-like behavior in your home. If so, that is wonderful, but if you have some lingering wounds, remember, you do not have to be stuck there. With God's help, any chains of bondage and pain can be broken, and you can live with a totally new identity—in Christ!

I will assume from now on you know you are a "Christ-follower" who desires to experience all God has for you. My goal is to give you tools to help you live an incredible, abundant, authentic, empowered, victorious life. Are you in? Let's go.

At the point of conversion, our life is transformed. We actually go through a metamorphosis, much like a butterfly. However, the green caterpillar morphs alone inside a cocoon while we are transformed mostly in a community. We cannot live our Christian life in isolation. This is *so* important. We are social creatures and need others to encourage us and also to help hold us accountable.

Think about the comparison here: To have a more abundant life requires morphing from what we were to what we become. A caterpillar and a butterfly share the same life, but by morphing, the butterfly reaches a "more abundant," experienced life. That change does not come about without tension or a struggle. Have you ever watched a butterfly emerge from a cocoon? It is not easy, but the butterfly must build up the endurance it needs to fly. It's a journey. We go through a similar process of struggle to learn how to live our new life in Christ. The important thing is we need to leave the cocoon behind. It is baggage and no longer a part of our life.

> *We cannot live our Christian life in isolation.*

We all long to become more, to become a better self. That's why self-help books and seminars have become a multibillion-dollar industry. Our God created us in His image, and we long to find what is missing.

What Happens When We Receive Christ as Our Savior?

What does it look like to have a changed life? It looks like a caterpillar becoming a butterfly.

First, we experience a "spiritual birth" in which we receive Christ's righteousness in exchange for our "sin." Then we activate our "spiritual growth" through which we progressively look like Him as we take on the family resemblance. Since we now have His spiritual seed within us with the new birth, all things are becoming new. We won't reach "spiritual maturity" until we meet Him face to face, but at that time, we will be like Him (1 John 3:2).

As we grow in this new life, it's okay to take baby steps. You know how it is when a toddler is learning how to walk. They take a few steps, and they fall. Do you scold them for falling? No, you encourage them to get up and try again to see if they will go farther the next time. They keep trying and falling until finally, they get it. God is the same way with us as we struggle to learn this new way of life. He is our biggest supporter and cheerleader all the way. We just need to be sure we are teachable and follow His lead.

During this process, it is essential to stop trying so hard, and allow Jesus to live His life through you, so your behavior and lifestyle match what is true. Try as you might, you can never perfectly imitate Christ. You will end up discouraged with failure time and time again. Just rest in Him and let Him do the work.

Paul, in Galatians 2:20, says of himself after his conversion: "I have been crucified with Christ. It is no longer I who live, but Christ who lives in me. And the life I now live in the flesh I live by faith in the Son of God, who loved me and gave Himself for me." This is true for any of us who have given our hearts to Jesus.

The only thing is, this liberating spirit only applies to the places where we relinquish control. If you are holding onto an area in your life and don't want to let go, you will not experience true freedom and victory. That only comes with complete and total surrender.

We will be talking a lot more about surrender later on, as that is *key* in experiencing the victorious life. We learn from 2 Corinthians 3:17, "Now the Lord is the Spirit, and where the Spirit of the Lord is, there is freedom."

LET'S TALK ABOUT FREEDOM

Freedom becomes our reality only when we yield entirely to God's authority. Again, if you knowingly hold out in any area of your life, you are not wholly free. Satan still has a hold on you in that area, which will hold you back from experiencing all you can in Christ.

Beware: Satan will do whatever it takes to convince you to say "No" to God. His very name means "one who separates." He is the deceiver (Revelation 12:9), who will try to convince you other "worldly choices" are better. Don't you believe it! You must be discerning. He has all kinds of tricks to pull you away. He will lull you into complacency, prideful self-sufficiency, or make you feel like you're not enough and a failure.

> *Freedom becomes our reality only when we yield entirely to God's authority.*

Our heart is the source of our actions in life, and it is through our thoughts that Satan plants his ideas and lies. He gets to us through images, feelings, and fears, and our actions come out of that. It is so subtle. He cannot force us to choose evil over good. That is a choice we have to make by deciding one decision or action is better than another. His tactics have not changed over all these generations. He works upon the heart through the mind—just like he did with Eve in the garden.

Don't let him get under your skin. While we are not capable of "perfect performance" this side of heaven, we are capable of "perfect love." We can choose to let God love through us and pursue a love relationship with Him above all else. Love originated with God, was manifested in His Son, and is demonstrated in His people like you and me.

We are told in Psalm 37:4, "Delight yourself in the LORD, and he will give you the desires of your heart." David wrote this psalm to encourage us to live in light of eternity and set our hope in God's eternal purposes—to align our hopes and desires with His. When we delight in Him and pledge ourselves to God's capable hands, our desire for virtue will prevail and be understood in His timing.

> *Love originated with God, was manifested in His Son, and is demonstrated in His people like you and me.*

As much as God wants to bless us, we have free choice, and He will not force Himself on anyone. If we continually, willfully disobey His precepts, He will let us suffer the consequences of our sin and give us over to our depraved minds as Paul describes in Romans 1.

God has to discipline us out of His love for us, just like we chastise our children. We often tell our children growing up if we didn't care how they turned out as adults, we wouldn't go through the agony of confrontation to discipline them. It's because we love them so much we step out of our comfort zone to correct them. We enforce restrictions, etc. so they learn inappropriate behavior cannot be tolerated.

This discipline is not because we want to be cruel; we hate doing it. Because of our life experience, we know if they are slothful, or we let them get away with inappropriate conduct or show disrespect toward authority growing up, they will have problems with teachers, employers, and eventually, God Himself. It is out of our love and desire for them to be successful in life, that we correct poor actions and attitudes, and endeavor to model lives of obedience.

> *God doesn't tell us He will give us a perfect mind if we are steadfast in Him, but He does tell us He will give us perfect peace in our imperfect minds.*

God doesn't tell us He will give us a perfect mind if we are steadfast in Him, but He does tell us He will give us perfect peace in our imperfect minds. "You keep him in perfect peace whose mind is stayed on you, because he trusts in you" (Isaiah 26:3),

The more we feed the Spirit of God within us and yield to His control, the more His presence will fill and satisfy us with life and peace. To *possess* a steadfast mind, we must *practice* a steadfast mind. We have believed too many lies that we are not enough and other misleading thoughts for far too long. Through the power of the Holy Spirit, we can take our thoughts captive instead.

> *Victorious lives flow from victorious thoughts, which comes from setting one's focus on a victorious God.*

We don't become victors by conquering or being independent of the enemy, but through our surrender to Christ and our dependence on God. Our road to success is a bit of a paradox. Those who experience freedom and victory are those whose minds are captivated by Christ. Victorious lives flow from victorious thoughts, which comes from setting one's focus on a victorious God. The only way to keep our thoughts from working against us is by intentionally keeping the focus where it should be—that He who is in us is greater than he who is in the world (1 John 4:4).

What Happens When We Receive Christ as Our Savior?

Reading His Word, we learn it tells us we are to confess our sins, repent, and embrace Jesus as our only hope of salvation. It goes on to say we are to deny ourselves, take up our cross daily, and follow Him in Matthew 16:24. We are to count the cost of following Him. While salvation is free for us, we need to remember it cost Jesus His life. God's moral law is something we need to take very seriously. It must become our passion.

> *The overwhelming evidence of the Holy Spirit in one's life is the distinctive family resemblance to Jesus Christ.*

The overwhelming evidence of the Holy Spirit in one's life is the distinctive family resemblance to Jesus Christ. Do people see Christ in you? As we go through the sanctification process, we become one with Jesus, so the same nature that controls Him controls us. It will cost everything in us, which is not of God. Are you ready for that?

Depending on one's current life status and cultural situation, there may be a tremendous cost, even persecution for making that kind of decision—for Christ. We must count the cost and be willing to submit and sacrifice whatever is necessary to accept the benefit of the ransom Jesus paid for us. All who live godly lives in the name of Jesus will suffer persecution of some sort. The Bible does not deny or distort reality or sugar coat expectations.

Those converting from other religions like Jews and Muslims are often shunned and rejected by their families. Still, they have weighed the cost and found Jesus well worth the sacrifice. Many Muslims who have embraced Christ have lost their lives by refusing to renounce their Christian faith. They are actual martyrs and exemplify incredible devotion and sacrifice. We need to realize if the *world* has nothing to say *against* us, *Jesus* may have nothing to say *for* us.

How are we to overcome persecution? Remember the words of Christ: "If the world hates you, know that it has hated me before it hated you" (John 15:18). "...Here on earth you will have many trials and sorrows. But take heart, because I have `overcome the world" (John 16:33 NLT).

Paul testifies that even though he was persecuted, the Lord never abandoned him; He stood by him, strengthened him, and delivered him from all his persecutions and infirmities (2 Corinthians 4:8–10). When we fully surrender to Christ, we will have the same testimony. We will learn as we go along; suffering can be redemptive. Sacrifice is necessary, but the rewards have eternal significance.

> *Our obedience evidences our love, and our passion for Christ is inseparable from our obedience.*

"Obedience" and "Surrender" are two words you will continuously see throughout this book. Victory in Christ is the result of those two ingredients. Now let's start unpacking that. The answer to liberty is to withhold nothing—no part of our lives from His authority and control. Obedience does not mean you have no sin or are perfect. When we *do* sin (and we *will* sin), we will need to confess and repent, trusting God will forgive.

Obedience does not mean living in a perpetual state of godliness but inviting the Spirit of God to flow freely through us as we learn to love, treasure, and act on God's Word. We cannot say we love God with all our hearts and, at the same time, live in willful disobedience. Our obedience evidences our love, and our passion for Christ is inseparable from our obedience.

What Happens When We Receive Christ as Our Savior?

While we're on the topic of surrender, let's address the importance of surrendering our thoughts to God. That is not only a means of experiencing a more consistent victory. It's also the safeguard against being given over to a depraved mind. That is where sin begins—in the mind. Wrong thoughts will lead to evil actions, which will result in negative consequences. What do we find when we look at Christ? We see absolute surrender to God. That was the very root of His life.

> *We can do the will of God only by the power of God.*

Our goal is to become like Jesus, right? What was His ultimate purpose in His earthly life?

- In the Garden of Gethsemane, He prayed, "...**your will be done**" (Matthew 26:42).

- He said, "My food is to **do the will of him who sent me** and to accomplish his work" (John 4:34).

- "For I have come down from heaven, **not to do my own will but the will of him who sent me**" (John 6:38).

We can do the will of God only by the power of God. How do *we* know God's will? He speaks to us through His Word and our conscious mind. Discernment comes with time as we learn to hear and recognize His voice above all the other noises in our head. It is an impression on our hearts. If we think we might be hearing from Him, it will help to ask these questions:

1. Does what I hear line up with Scripture?
2. Does it seem consistent with His character?
3. Am I being drawn to similar ideas/thoughts through messages, or when studying during quiet time?
4. Am I being led to do something beyond me, so that God would get the credit?
5. Is it something that would please God or give Him glory?

Even though rejection, suffering, and shame were part of His God-given experience, Christ accepted everything God set before Him to do because He knew and trusted His Father's heart. As we look throughout Scripture, we can see time and again, obedience leads to freedom, while rebellion leads to slavery every time. It appears we have two choices: We can choose to be a slave to a loving God who always looks out for our best interests, or we can be a slave to sin. To me, this is a "no-brainer."

If, by chance, you are still struggling with satisfaction in your life, let's look at what might be hindering you so you can ask God to remove it. Usually, it is a result of refusing Him access to a particular area of one's life. It could be there is something in your life you need to confess and straighten out. Be careful. If you ever find yourself being too proud to admit something, you can expect mercy, or answers to your prayers will be hindered.

> *Obedience leads to freedom, while rebellion leads to slavery every time.*

Just because Jesus saved you, which indeed was a gift from God, that does not necessarily mean you will be satisfied. That is unless you have deliberately let the fullness of Christ fill and control every area of your life. Satisfaction is a byproduct of salvation, and God intended it for every believer.

Walking consistently with God, pursuing daily obedience is the best way I know to fulfill His ideal plans for us. We will not walk perfectly. No doubt, we will stumble, but we will not fall. When we declare our love for the Lord and submit our life to Him, He will not only bless and guide us but also bring a sense of genuine fulfillment to our hearts.

One thing I can guarantee you, the more you come to know God and camp out on His attributes and promises as outlined in the Bible, the more you will want to get to know Him. The more time you intentionally spend with Him in prayer, worship, and reading His Word, the more you will yearn for Him. Your response to the Word of God will determine your relationship with Him. Once you taste and see how good the Lord is, you will be ravenous for more of Him (Psalm 34:8).

> *Your response to the Word of God will determine your relationship with Him.*

We need to be careful about our motivation for Bible study and especially prayer. If we are not careful, our focus could still be "all about me" and how God can improve our circumstances. Although our requests could sincerely be about good things such as power and success in ministry, wisdom, and direction to do the right things, etc., our motivation may not be to seek God's will and guidance. As much as God desires to hear and answer our petitions, His greatest joy is to receive them from a heart longing for Him more than anything He could give us.

Diving Deeper

1. What, or who was most instrumental in helping you to give your life to Christ? Explain.

2. Before reading this chapter, did you think that much about where you found your identity? Has that now changed?

3. What are some outward signs others should be able to see when one gives their life to Christ?

4. Debby said spiritual training begins with personal integrity. What does that mean to you? How are you doing with that? What do you need to change?

5. How would you summarize the main points of this chapter?

6. What was the most impactful Scripture verse in this chapter, and why?

7. In what ways are you already challenged in this book to make significant changes in your life? What are they?

8. Debby challenged each of us to work at achieving the fruit of the Spirit in our lives. How do you plan to accomplish that?

9. What are some ways we can test to be sure we are being led by the Holy Spirit to carry out God's will?

10 What steps do you need to take to intentionally live a more grateful, joyful life, making more godly choices?

Chapter 2

Can We Lose Our Salvation?

Before I move on to the meat of this book, I want to take a few minutes to answer a question I have a feeling might come up in the back of your mind. I know some people wonder if they can ever lose their salvation. This question usually comes up when someone struggles in their walk, maybe with temptation or Satan's attack in any number of ways. You might be wondering because of the "bad" or "lack" of fruit you see in yourself or someone else you thought was a Christian.

Let me remind you of a famous parable. Are you familiar with the parable of the seeds and the different kinds of soil, as told by Jesus in Matthew 13:3–8?

> A sower went out to sow. And as he sowed, some seeds fell along the path, and the birds came and devoured them. Other seeds fell on rocky ground, where they did not have much soil, and immediately they sprang up, since they had no depth of soil, but when the sun rose they were scorched. And since they had no root, they withered away. Other seeds fell among thorns, and the thorns grew up and choked them. Other seeds fell on good soil and produced grain, some a hundredfold, some sixty, some thirty.

He then explained the parable in verses 18–23,

> Hear then the parable of the sower: When anyone hears the word of the kingdom and does not understand

it, the evil one comes and snatches away what has been sown in his heart. This is what was sown along the path. As for what was sown on rocky ground, this is the one who hears the word and immediately receives it with joy, yet he has no root in himself, but endures for a while, and when tribulation or persecution arises on account of the word, immediately he falls away. As for what was sown among thorns, this is the one who hears the word, but the cares of the world and the deceitfulness of riches choke the word, and it proves unfruitful. As for what was sown on good soil, this is the one who hears the word and understands it. He indeed bears fruit and yields, in one case a hundredfold, in another sixty, and in another thirty.

Unfortunately, for many people, they fall into one of the first three categories, and they never were redeemed. A story or experience may have moved them. They may have even responded to an altar call. Still, redemption never took root, meaning salvation was not secured in the first place. We might call them "backsliders"; however, true repentance did not occur in these instances. As long as the seed fell on good soil and grew, one is secure in their salvation; but there may need to be a "heart-check" as to the status of that surrender if our outward lives are not reflecting our inward belief.

Let's look at yourself for a moment. Who/what is the number one priority in your life? Do you believe lies about not being enough, etc.? Satan is an expert at stealthfully deceiving us of all kinds of lies about ourselves. If that's the case, you only need to confess your struggle to Jesus, who will forgive you and help you get back on track. God will never turn down a genuinely repentant heart.

Ask the Holy Spirit to reveal anything you need to confess to getting right with God. Then just sit and listen. Then confess and turn it over to Him. I have found that starting with praise to God for many of His attributes helps to get me in the right frame of mind. (I have created a partial list of those in the Appendix for your reference.) I love to listen to uplifting Christian music as well. Sometimes, we just need to unplug from worldly distractions and plug into God to get us back on track.

I became a Christian at a very young age, but was brought up in a denomination that did not teach about assurance of salvation or "eternal security." I thought I needed to ask Jesus into my heart continually. To be sure I was covered, I would sing the song, "Lord, I Want to be a Christian in My Heart," every night when I went to bed. (Kind of like saying the prayer, "Now I lay me down to sleep.")

When I was a sophomore in high school, and I visited my Uncle's church, the Sunday school teacher asked me if I had ever asked Jesus into my heart. I told her, "Oh, I do that every night."

She said, "Honey, you don't have to do that! You only have to ask Him once. He will never leave you!"

Wow, was that ever good news! That is what I want to tell you today. Once you have sincerely turned your life over to Christ, He will never leave you nor forsake you (Hebrews 13:5). John 10:27-28 tells us, "My sheep hear My voice, and I know them, and they follow Me. I give them eternal life, and they will never perish, and no one will snatch them out of My hand."

> *One incredible fact regarding our salvation in Christ is it is irreversible; that is, no one can undo what God has done.*

One incredible fact regarding our salvation in Christ is it is irreversible; that is, no one can undo what God has done. Once God truly saves us, He secures our salvation forever because our salvation has at its basis the very nature and person of God Himself. Jesus tells us in John 15:16, "You did not choose me, but I chose you..."

Salvation was God's idea, not ours. He pursued each of us until we responded. I have never quite gotten over the cross, the sacrifice that took place there, and the fact Jesus "chose" me. He chose you as well! Can you believe that? What a fantastic gift.

> *No sin, failure, or weakness on our part can separate us from the love of God or cause Him to love us any less.*

Jesus knows our sins very well; however, He did not come to rub them in, but to rub them out. He did not come to condemn or shame us, but to save and change us. Isn't that mind-blowing love!

This unbelievable act of love is what drew me to Christ when I was a child. My mom used to read me Bible stories at bedtime, and I was so overwhelmed with the crucifixion story that I repeatedly asked her to read it to me over and over again. I could not comprehend that someone would take the punishment I deserved and die for me in such a horrific death so that I could live forever with God in heaven.

I didn't even understand about the wrath of God or human rejection at that point, but I certainly understood physical pain. How could I *not* love someone like that? I have loved Jesus ever since.

Have I always been obedient to Him once I started studying the Bible and learning how a Christian was supposed to look and act? Absolutely not! Like anyone else, I have struggled to surrender particular weaknesses and vulnerabilities to Him.

In fact, for a while, I thought I was doing pretty well in my walk with the Lord when I would compare myself to others I knew—even godly friends. Then, with the Holy Spirit's help, who convicts us when we are wrong, I realized I was using the wrong metric. I was supposed to compare myself to Christ, not other sinners.

I will say, the more serious I have become in following Christ and asking Him to show me what it looks like to be totally surrendered to Him, the more the "sin quotient" in my life has substantially diminished. I'm a slow learner, and I still fail at times, but I have finally learned what it takes to live a victorious Christian life, and that is what I want to share with you within these pages. There is nothing like it, and I want more than anything for you to experience it!

> *Our salvation is grounded in a God who is unchanging in His love and faithfulness toward us.*

It was He who called us, so He plans to keep us. There is no way He would call us unto salvation and then abandon us. God's salvation is eternal. One lesson we can learn from the book of Job (in the Old Testament) is, no matter what Satan does, nothing can destroy saving faith.

Additionally, God's love and grace toward us are not restricted or temporary. He loves us with an undying love. When Christ loves us, it is to the fullest. No sin, failure, or weakness on our part can separate us from the love of God or cause Him to love us any less. Isn't that incredible?

"For I am sure that neither death nor life, nor angels nor rulers, nor things present nor things to come, nor powers, nor height nor depth, nor anything else in all creation, will be able to separate us from the love of God in Christ Jesus our Lord" (Romans 8:38–39)

As Jonah in the Old Testament found out, even if we wanted to run away from God, it would be impossible. If it were possible to lose our salvation, many of us would have already, based on our sins, and our sometimes erratic thoughts and feelings. Thankfully, our salvation is grounded in a God who is unchanging in His love and faithfulness toward us. If He loved us enough to save us, He surely loves us enough to keep us. If we ever feel far from God, it's because we have turned our back and moved away from Him, not the converse. He never deserts us. Even though we often are unfaithful, great is His faithfulness!

Unfortunately, we are living in an age of spiritual illiteracy, which has contributed to many confused, shallow spiritual lives, wherein even Christians don't understand the process of transformation and have no idea how to grow spiritually. This ignorance results in spiritual failure with the inability to "walk by faith." That would require knowing enough about what the Bible says to recognize "life alerts" from Scripture.

If you look over the "Obstacles to Grace" (next chapter), you may find yourself there. You might see how Satan may have pulled you away from your "First Love," and you need to work that out with God. It does not mean you have lost your salvation. Maybe you have just lost the "joy" of your salvation and the ability to experience intimacy with your true love, and that is why you feel the way you do. Remember, our salvation is based on God, not on us. Life-change is both a gift from God and also a responsibility. Only God can change our life, but He chooses not to do it alone. This is not a passive activity. We *do* have a responsibility to be obedient to God and His Word through which we validate our surrender. Then we will see growth.

> *Even though we often are unfaithful, great is His faithfulness!*

Let me give you an example. If you plant a flower, you cannot make it grow. Only God can do that. But if you provide the proper environment with water, fertilizer, and plant it where it will receive sufficient sun, it will flourish. Spiritual growth works much the same way. Only God can provide your growth. Either you can stifle it, *or* choose to cooperate, making the conditions in your life favorable, making growth possible. So if you are feeling distant from God, a heart check may be in order. Once the broken fellowship is restored, you are on your way to experiencing the victorious life you always wanted.

DIVING DEEPER

1. Have you ever wondered about your salvation? If so, what made you question it?

2. If we could lose our salvation, what would that say about Jesus's promises about salvation? What are some verses to support that?

3. When have you felt the farthest from God? What has helped to pull you back on track and return to fellowship with Him?

4. Has there ever been a time when you experienced the enemy trying to pull you down and tell you that you don't matter, that God doesn't love you, or you aren't really saved? Explain.

5. As you look over the priorities in your life, who is your first love, and what makes you think that way? As you think about people and things in your life that are important to you, do you think you need to reprioritize anything going forward? Explain.

6. Can you summarize the parable of the seeds, as explained in Matthew 13:3-23? Where do you see yourself? Can you see where a change maybe has occurred in your life over time? Explain.

7 .Are there people in your life who you see fall in one of the first three categories? If so, are you committed to diving deeper into this study to see how you can be instrumental in helping them see the truth of the gospel? How would you go about that?

8. What is/are your favorite verse(s) in this chapter, and why?

9. What was the primary truth of this chapter, and what lesson(s) do you see?

10. What new/encouraging/challenging points stand out to you in this chapter?

Chapter 3

Obstacles to Grace

What are obstacles that could be keeping you from experiencing the victorious Christian life? The issues I present in this chapter certainly do not constitute an exhaustive list, and they are not in any particular order. As I look over these obstacles, though, I see they are all internal issues except the last one, generational bondage, which becomes a mindset based on one's experience. We need to look at our thought life as well as our hearts and guard them against these destructive issues.

As mentioned earlier, when we become a Christ-follower, we receive the Holy Spirit into our lives. He lives in our hearts and minds. He cannot function around garbage. He can help us get rid of it, but cannot endure that sustained environment. Can you imagine being productive if you had to live in a room full of stinky garbage 24/7? I will be discussing later how God calls us to be holy, pure, and perfect. Living this kind of life is possible through the Holy Spirit's power in our lives, but only if we let Him clean house first. Let's be sure we are not quenching His Spirit, robbing us of this supernatural power available to us.

> *If we are not overcoming temptations, the world and its sordid attractions will overwhelm us.*

Each of these obstacles listed below is considered a sin, which keeps us from experiencing God's grace and His best. We all will succumb to any one or more of these at some point in our life; however, as a Christ-follower, none of these should be habitual. What's scary about sin is we tend to get accustomed to it gradually, so it becomes addictive, and we finally come to the place where we no longer even realize it is sin.

> *There is no temptation unless first, there was a desire.*

No power, except what comes with the Holy Spirit, can change or prevent the natural consequences of sin. One devastating effect of unrepentant sin is it dulls your senses, leaving you spiritually blind and deaf.

We need to recognize our vulnerability, repent, and confess any shortcomings, and ask the Holy Spirit to help us flee, stand up to, and overcome future temptations. If we are not overcoming temptations, the world and its sordid attractions will overwhelm us.

We cannot blame our desires on temptations. It's actually the other way around. There is no temptation unless first, there was a desire. From where do our desires come? Usually, they are a result of something we lack, something we wished we had but don't. Desire brings along temptation. James 1:14-15 tells us: "But each person is tempted when he is lured and enticed by his own desire. Then desire when it has conceived gives birth to sin, and sin, when it is fully grown, brings forth death."

> *We must be careful what we let our eyes see and our ears hear since they are intricately connected to our hearts and minds.*

You might say, "That doesn't tempt me in the least" for some things. That's because you had no desire for it, whereas other things might tempt you because there is an inner desire causing an internal struggle. We must be careful what we let our eyes see and our ears hear since they are intricately connected to our hearts and minds.

Temptation itself if not a sin. It's what we do with the temptation that matters. Do we act on it, or walk away? Remember, 1 Corinthians 10:13 tells us: "No temptation has overtaken you that is not common to man. God is faithful, and he will not let you be tempted beyond your ability, but with the temptation he will also provide the way of escape, that you may be able to endure it."

We will never be able to walk closely with God unless we see sin as He does.

We need to hate sin as God does and not allow anything in our home, relationships, or minds that could lead us to sin. We will never be able to walk closely with God unless we see sin as He does. Darkness and light cannot coexist, but light always overcomes darkness. Run from the darkness into the light! We need to be aware of all the areas we are tempted to sin so we can be mindful of our vulnerabilities and ask God to help us in these areas.

- **Pride** has to lead the list of obstacles to grace, holiness, and victory in the Christian life. It can taint or destroy almost anything good, and because it is so damaging, it is dangerous. It is the root of most sin and the total antithesis to humility, as modeled by Christ. We can find examples throughout the New Testament, where Jesus showed ultimate humility and servant leadership. Pride often leads to arrogance, which is good for nothing. It comes so naturally we have to fight it intentionally. We must remember: "Pride goes before destruction and a haughty spirit before a fall" (Proverbs 16:18). Also, "God opposes the proud but gives grace to the humble" (James 4:6).

- **Unbelief** rates right up there with pride. It does not necessarily mean a lack of belief in God, but lack of trust that He can and will carry out what He says He'll do. It is a lack of faith. This lack of faith is a byproduct of not knowing God. Paul reminds us in 2 Timothy 1:12: "I know whom I have believed, and I am convinced that he is able to guard until that day what has been entrusted to me."

- **Unforgiveness toward others** – If we think we cannot forgive others, we have honestly forgotten what happened at the cross. Are we so much better than Christ, we cannot/will not forgive others after what Christ has done for us? I would include bitterness and resentment in this category as they are probably a byproduct of an unforgiving attitude.

Unforgiveness indeed interferes with intimacy with God. Do you feel like your prayers are going nowhere? Look to see if there is anyone you need to forgive. Unforgiveness creates a chasm that definitely would inhibit one from experiencing a victorious life. I direct you to the parable of the unmerciful servant in Matthew 19:21–35. Forgiveness is so important I have devoted a whole chapter to it.

- **Unforgiveness of self** – Many times, we have trouble forgiving ourselves for something we have done in the past, and we forget that when we repent, God forgives us. It is history He chooses to forget and does not hold against us. Knowing God has forgiven us, we must forgive ourselves. It serves no useful purpose to continue to beat up on ourselves. "For I will be merciful toward their iniquities, and I will remember their sins no more" (Hebrews 8:12).

Let's remember we should follow Paul's example in not being constrained by past sins, as stated in Philippians 3:13: "Brothers, I do not consider that I have made it on my own. But one thing I do: forgetting what lies behind and straining forward to what lies ahead."

- **Idolatry** is anything we might put in place of God regarding the priority of our affections. When we put our desire before the Designer, that is idolatry. He must come first. If we are putting anything, like our spouse, children, status, career, finances, even ministry before our love for God, then that is idolatry, which hinders our walk. God must be our first love. "You shall have no other gods before me" (Exodus 20:3).

- **Spiritual Ignorance** – Lack of knowledge. This is why Bible study is *so* important! We must study the Bible to know the truth and be aware of any false teaching. "Jesus said to them, 'Is this not the reason you are wrong, because you know neither the Scriptures nor the power of God?'" (Mark 12:24). "As obedient children, do not be conformed to the passions of your former ignorance" (1 Peter 1:14).

- **Prayerlessness** – Prayerless lives are powerless lives, while prayerful lives are powerful. We cannot enjoy or experience the presence of God without spending time with Him in prayer. Prayer is huge. Not praying is also like telling God you don't need His help. On the other hand, He loves to answer the prayers of His children who ask in faith, seeking His will. He loves for us to depend on and lean into Him. It also allows us to see where God is already working and inviting us to join Him. I have devoted a whole chapter to this as well. "The prayer of a righteous person has great power as it is working" (James 5:16).

- **Jealousy** – Not being content with what God has given. As Christ-followers, we need to trust God to meet all our needs and be not only content but also grateful. Jealousy could be the result of coveting something someone else has. Paul said: "Not that I am speaking of being in need, for I have learned in whatever situation I am to be content" (Philippians 4:11). "And my God will supply every need of yours according to his riches in glory in Christ Jesus" (Philippians 4:19).

- **Spiritual Isolation** – Self-dependency—self-reliance. We cannot live out our faith on our own. We have to be in a relationship with others to walk out our faith. That is where the true testing of our faith is. "Not that we are sufficient in ourselves to claim anything as coming from us, but our sufficiency is from God" (2 Corinthians 3:5). "And let us consider how to stir up one another to love and good works, not neglecting to meet together, as is the habit of some, but encouraging one another, and all the more as you see the Day drawing near" (Hebrews 10:24–25).

- **Legalism** – This word is not actually in the Bible but is alluded to a lot with many examples. It describes those who are dependent on rules. If you remember, Jesus often healed on the Sabbath. The Pharisees were upset that He appeared to be working on the Sabbath, saying Jesus was breaking the law by healing someone. Legalism is when we put rules and regulations before relationships and performance before passion. You don't see grace in legalism. "For by grace you have been saved through faith. And this is not your own doing; it is the gift of God, not a result of works, so that no one may boast" (Ephesians 2:8–9).

- **Fear** – shows a lack of faith and trust in God. Sometimes, there is even fear if we fully surrender to God, He will require something of us that will make us unhappy or require us to step out of our comfort zone, making us miserable. Fear also shows a lack of trust that He has our best interest in mind. It's okay to have some trepidation when He calls us to do something; however, we must not get stuck there. Instead, we need to have the courage to step out in faith to accomplish what God calls us to do. When we become a child of God, we are no longer slaves

OBSTACLES TO GRACE

to fear. "For God gave us a spirit not of fear but of power and love and self-control" (2 Timothy 1:7).

- **Doubts accompanied by skepticism** – believing lies is often accompanied by discouragement (Satan's best tool). It's okay to have questions and concerns while seeking the truth. It's a matter of attitude and mindset when doubts come. "Be sober-minded; be watchful. Your adversary, the devil, prowls around like a roaring lion, seeking someone to devour" (1 Peter 5:8). When our faith is tested, it reveals what is in our heart and has the potential to produce a robust faith.

- **Grieving or quenching the Spirit** - Knowingly/intentionally ignoring or going against the Spirits promptings: "Do not quench the Spirit" (1 Thessalonians 5:19). We must be careful about this one. If we ignore (quench or grieve) the Spirit consistently, He will go silent, and we will no longer benefit from His presence. He will always be there but remain dormant if we don't continually ask for His filling and respond to His promptings.

- **Yielding to the temptation to sin** - When one is not guarding one's heart and mind, leading to inappropriate desires, it is easy to follow temptation into sin. "Let no one say when he is tempted, 'I am being tempted by God,' for God cannot be tempted with evil, and he himself tempts no one. But each person is tempted when he is lured and enticed by his own desire. Then desire when it has conceived gives birth to sin, and sin when it is fully grown brings forth death" (James 1:13-16).

- **Blaming others rather than taking responsibility for our actions** – Finger-pointing is rampant. No one wants to admit personal failure. Accusations started back in the Garden of Eden. There is no place for blame-shifting in the abundant Christian life. "Why do you see the speck that is in your brother's eye, but do not notice the log that is in your own eye? Or how can you say to your brother, 'Let me take the speck out of your eye,' when there is the log in your own eye? You hypocrite, first take the log out of your own eye, and then you will see clearly to take the speck out of your brother's eye" (Matthew 7:3–5).

- **Being sucked into the world system –** The culture which ignores or rebels against God and His ways can pull your thoughts and actions in a direction that is inconsistent with who you are in Christ. We become like those we hang out with, so choose your friends carefully. As a side note and food for thought: if you spend a lot of time with God in prayer and His Word, just think of the person you would most likely come to imitate! Wow, talk about transformation! "Submit yourselves therefore to God. Resist the devil, and he will flee from you" (James 4:7).

- **Lack of Faith –** If we cannot believe in the inerrancy of the Word of God or the truth of God's promises, we certainly will never experience a victorious life rooted in the faithfulness of a truthful, loving God. Genuine faith will always produce authentic obedience. Faith in no way eliminates our problems but helps us trust God in the midst of them. Nothing pleases God more than when we exercise faith—trusting and believing in Him. The only time Jesus rebuked His disciples was for their unbelief. "Jesus immediately reached out His hand and took hold of him, saying to him, 'O you of little faith, why did you doubt?'" (Matthew 14:31). "And without faith, it is impossible to please him, for whoever would draw near to God must believe that he exists and that he rewards those who seek him" (Hebrews 11:6).

- **Spiritual Myopia –** Short-sightedness—Unable to see the big picture. Those with spiritual myopia have a bent toward negativity, bitterness, and loss of perspective with a tendency to blame others (often God) for their misery. The cure consists of a daily dose of gratitude for what one has and has received rather than what may have been lost. "For whoever lacks these qualities is so nearsighted that he is blind, having forgotten that he was cleansed from his former sins" (2 Peter 1:9).

- **Generational Bondage does not have to be your legacy.** You can break the chains of iniquity in your heritage. With God's help, you do not have to be in bondage to anything. "And you will know the truth, and the truth will set you free" (John 8:32).

God wants us to experience His joy, but that is not possible unless we mourn over our sin. If we don't grieve over the weight of our sin, it shows we have no concept or sense of its devastating power or the enormity of our offense against God.

God wants us to experience His joy, but that is not possible unless we mourn over our sin.

Confession is not necessarily an indication of repentance. There can only be true repentance when we realize the gravity of our sin. Regret for the consequences of our sinning is not the same as sorrow for sinning against God. We must acknowledge and be heartbroken that our sin has come from a heart out of tune with God. We must recognize the gravity of our transgressions against a holy God.

I will get real here because it matters. If you do not get habitual sin under control, you will inevitably quench the Spirit of God in you, and not experience God's fullness. Whenever you yield to something, you will realize—if you haven't already—it has tremendous control over you. We are a slave to what we say, "yes" to. You will find the habit dominates you because you willingly yielded to it. Taking whatever steps are

> *We are a slave to what we say, "Yes" to.*

necessary to overcome whatever obstacles are in your life should be your number one priority. If you want God to use you to produce the fruit of a godly legacy—if you want your life to count for God—you must tap into the Holy Spirit's power to help you overcome habitual sin.

Ravi Zacharias, the late famous theologian, often quoted the old adage, "Sin will take you further than you want to go, keep you longer than you want to stay, and cost you more than you want to pay."

God wants so much to make us whole, which often means breaking destructive habits. When we butterflies act like caterpillars, refusing to leave the cocoon behind, it breaks His heart. His call to holiness isn't about a bunch of rules. He wants to protect us from ourselves.

If you are struggling with some addiction, please find a Christian accountability partner who cares about you, will speak the truth, and will not enable you in your addiction. Then get professional Christian help. Otherwise, this sin will devour you. You must get serious about this with a desire to be delivered and get honest with God about overcoming this obstacle. The freedom you experience once you gain victory over this will be life-changing, and it will be eternally worthwhile.

> *"Sin will take you further than you want to go, keep you longer than you want to stay, and cost you more than you want to pay."*

Willpower will not work. The pull is too strong. You must be at the point where you are desperate and broken with a real desire to come clean. Ask God for the grace and power to overcome. God always gives grace to the humble.

Not to be too dramatic or judgmental, but truthful—if others are aware of your sin and know you profess to be a Christian, just think of what a poor example and negative witness this is to others who don't yet know Christ.

God always gives grace to the humble.

I know that is not your heart. Deep down, just because you're reading this book, I know you must want more of God and to experience the peace, joy, love, and power of a victorious life. This life is possible and within reach but will take some effort on your part as well as surrender and sacrifice, but the rewards will be well worth it. In so doing, you will please God with your life, and He can then use you to draw others to Him. Just think of what a positive, powerful testimony your life of redemption could be as people witness the transformation in your life.

Besides getting an accountability partner and Christian professional help, which are imperative, add to that diligently immersing yourself in God's Word, especially the New Testament with fervor, will result in a transformed heart over time—guaranteed!

How do we overcome these obstacles? We will be covering this in greater detail in the following chapters, but in a nutshell, we must put on Christ (Romans 13:14) by being crucified with Him (Galatians 2:20), dying to self (Mark 8:34–35), and being obedient to Him (John 14:21).

While in prison chained to Roman guards, Paul examined the armor of the Roman soldiers and used that as a metaphor to teach us how to put on the full armor of God described in Ephesians 6:10-18 to fight off the enemy. In addition to using this armor, James urges us to stay in community with other believers who can encourage us while also holding us accountable (James 5:16).

We need to remember no matter what difficulty or obstacle we might face, Jesus has already won the victory over the enemy who is the author and mastermind of all these obstacles. You do not need to live in defeat. You can be an overcomer and experience the victorious life—the life you always wanted!

Diving Deeper

1. What would you describe/define as an obstacle? A sin? Where do they come from?

2. Discuss grace and how obstacles interfere with experiencing grace and the abundant Christian life.

3. As you look at these obstacles listed here, which one(s) do you struggle with the most? Can you think of others not listed here that are a common handicap for those struggling in their walk with Christ? Please share.

4. How would your life look different if you could overcome these?

5. How do we overcome these obstacles? Who can help with that?

6. What verse(s) stand out as being most helpful for you? Why?

7. What is one interesting fact you learned in this chapter? The key point?

8. What does God's Word offer as counsel of how to fight against these desires/temptations?

9. In your own words, summarize the points made in this chapter.

10. How do you plan to apply what you have learned? What changes would you like to see in your life?

Chapter 4

What Is the Victorious Life And How Do We Live It?

Victory will undoubtedly look different to a believer than a non-believer. If you were to ask a non-believer what success and victory look like it, the response would probably be something like getting to the top of a corporate ladder, winning a big race or competition, or getting into the college of their choice. A football player would probably tell you that winning the super bowl would be the ultimate victory. Many individuals who have accomplished each of those milestones have acknowledged afterward, they often thought to themselves, "Is that all there is?"

For the Christian, it looks very different. The victorious Christian life is lived, by faith, in a moment-by-moment surrender and obedience to God. It is a life rooted and grounded in faith and surrender. True saving faith produces obedience and submission to the Lordship of Jesus Christ—the only thing that fills the God-shaped vacuum in our lives. One thing for sure—the victorious life is not is a mirage. It certainly is obtainable, sustainable, and eternal.

A victorious Christian life is living the *abundant* life—a beautiful life. The words themselves ring with hope. One caveat I must mention up front, though—don't be deceived. The "victorious life" does NOT mean a "worry-free" or "trouble-free" life. It could even be a much more challenging life, at least in the beginning. However, the good news is you do not have to live it on your own. You will have the most excellent helper possible to get you through it. Is it possible to live an abundant, "joy-filled" life—the life you always wanted—even when facing adversity? Absolutely! There is no other life like it this side of heaven. Let's talk about how.

When there is victory, then that implies something has been defeated. Our lives are usually made up of many small victories as we overcome various sins in our lives, which will be different for each of us as we all have our weaknesses and vulnerabilities.

WHAT IS VICTORY IN THE LIFE OF A CHRISTIAN?

It is a life of victory over sin. Is that even possible? There is no way we can be sinless like Christ. First John 1:8 tells us: "If we say we have no sin, we deceive ourselves, and the truth is not in us."

The victorious life is also a life of holiness/perfection. Now, before you might jump to the conclusion there is no way you could ever achieve holiness, let alone perfection, let's put that idea aside for now as I will explain this as we go along. It's not as idealistic or "out of reach" as is seems. Let's try to put away any preconceived ideas we may have about that, acknowledging upfront "we" in our strength anyway, will never be perfect in this life.

The more you love Jesus, your affections and desires change so much, you will be dealing with much less sin in your life.

We all have "known" sins in our life—sins with which we continually struggle. I want to encourage you; anything is possible with God. That is the key, and so I repeat, "With man this is impossible, with God all things are possible" (Matthew 19:26).

He is the key element. We can try to overcome even the smallest sins on our own, but we are incapable without His help through the Holy Spirit's power. You will find as we unpack all this, the more you love Jesus, your affections and desires change so much, you will be dealing with much less sin in your life. Doesn't that sound encouraging?

If you struggle with what you might call "small sins," when they are habitual, they rob you of your fellowship with God. If you are a Christ-follower, then you have been forgiven of all your sins—past, present, and future. But we must confess our known sins continually to have fellowship with the Father. If you continue to sin, especially in a particular area, it's essential to take extraordinary measures in prayer to ask the Holy Spirit to give you the strength to overcome and stand up against those temptations.

The writer of Hebrews reminds us of God's availability to help us, "Let us then with confidence draw near to the throne of grace, that we may receive mercy and find grace to help in time of need" (Hebrews 4:16). We are called to be faithful. The writer to the Hebrews continues in 12:1, saying we are to "lay aside every weight, and sin which clings so closely, and let us run with endurance the race that is set before us," Keep in mind the race is *not* something *we* choose or set up; it is chosen and "set before us."

The Greek word used for sin here is not referring to "sin" in general.[1] It is talking about a *particular* sin. It could be any sin or temptation that holds us back. Most scholars think he was referring *here* to the sin of unbelief—not trusting God completely, not relying on Him. That kind of belief and trust begins by "surrendering" to Him.

It's not so much a matter of "not" trusting God so much as we love "our way" so much that we "miss" His. In truth, there is this four-letter word that gets in the way: **"S-E-L-F"** that resists any thoughts of "surrender."

How *do* we surrender, release our grip, and truly rely on God? The next verse (vs. 2 of Hebrews 12) gives us the answer: "Looking to Jesus, the founder and perfecter of our faith, who for the joy that was set before him endured the cross, despising the shame, and is seated at the right hand of the throne of God."

We practice the discipline of surrender when we focus our attention on Jesus. Jesus is not *just* the prize at the finish line. He is also the example of how to run the race. He didn't just design the course of the race. He ran it, and ran it perfectly, relying on and trusting in the Father all along the way. We are to look to Him as the ultimate example of a life of surrender.

> *Jesus is not just the prize at the finish line. He is also the example of how to run the race.*

He came to the world He created and lived His entire life misunderstood, misrepresented, misquoted, mistreated, and finally crucified. Yet, He did not sin. From the manger to the cross, Jesus exemplified a life of obedience and surrender. The next time you feel unfairly treated, judged, criticized, or misunderstood, remember what Christ endured and keep Him as your standard. If you ever feel like you are being asked to surrender too much, remember what Jesus sacrificed and surrendered for you.

The good news is, when we learn how to live surrendered lives, trusting and relying on Jesus, we become more like Him. That is our goal, isn't it? We accomplish this by intentionally and deliberately working toward unselfishness, recognizing selfishness, and the pride that often accompanies it can be our most significant obstacle to reaching that goal.

Focusing intently on Christ and studying His example naturally results in a lifestyle of greater and greater selflessness. Another benefit of resting in Him—surrendering, is the peace we can experience in life's storms when we otherwise would experience chaos.

>
> I have always loved the old hymn:
>
> *"Turn your eyes upon Jesus.*
>
> *Look full in His wonderful face;*
>
> *And the things of earth will grow strangely dim*
>
> *In the light of His glory and grace."*

It's a win-win. Yes, we may have to give up our old ways, but His ways are always better!

A vast portion of the New Testament focuses on how to live a victorious life following Christ's example of perfect love, humility, and servant leadership. After Jesus's death, Paul, the apostle who wrote over half of the New Testament, gives incredible examples applying Jesus's teachings to our everyday life. If we want to grasp God's heart, the content of the book of Philippians is a great one to assimilate into our lives as well as Galatians, Ephesians, and Colossians. Paul wrote all of these while he was in prison.

> *Our goal as a "Christ-follower" is to become like Christ and be filled with all the fullness of God.*

When we experience victory in overcoming the sin in our life, we also experience the byproduct of *peace* (which passes all understanding), an inner *joy* (unspeakable), and also the very *power* (of God) to accomplish anything within His will. Christ offers us PJP (Peace, Joy, and Power).

Our goal as a "Christ-follower" is to become like Christ and be filled with all the fullness of God. We can do this only because He now lives inside of us and (as much as we let Him) lives His life through us. His desire and plan when we put our trust in Him are to dwell in our hearts and live His life in and through us. What a beautiful thing that is! Paul, in Philippians 2:13, sums up this great privilege in a sentence: "For it is God who works in you, both to will and to work for his good pleasure."

When we allow Christ to live His life through us, remember, it is not an "influence" or a "spiritual force." It is God Himself who dwells in the heart of every believer. We enter into Christ, and He enters into us. Paul tells us in Philippians 1:21: "For me to live is Christ…" and in Colossians 3:4: "Christ who is your life…"

How Does Christ Come to Live Inside Us as the Holy Spirit?

Now would be as good a time as any to try to explain the Trinity. This is complicated to grasp, but I will try to explain briefly what the Trinity is: The Three-in-one Godhead—one God in three forms with different functions. If you were to try to use math to explain it, the equation would not be 1+1+1=3 but 1 x 1 x 1=1.

There is God the Father, God the Son, and God the Holy Spirit. The word "Tri" means three, and the word "unity" means one. God is only one but in the form of three Persons who have the same essence of deity. Because they are three in one, we tend to use each name interchangeably.

Jesus was in the beginning with God but left the glory of heaven to come to earth to save us from our sin by taking it upon Himself to receive God's wrath in our place. Then, when He went back to the Father, He sent the Holy Spirit to point us to Himself and empower us to fulfill God's will as He reveals it to us.

Jesus declared it was to our advantage that He go back to the Father so we could experience the power of the Holy Spirit in each of our lives when we turn our life over to Christ. He indwells the heart of every believer.

There is no way we can live out God's will for our lives without the Holy Spirit's power. He *indwells* us as a believer, but we must continually ask Him to *fill* us with His power. It is when we launch out on our own and try to control the outcome we fail. We desperately need Him.

There's a lot of truth to the old hymn, "I Need Thee Every Hour." The Holy Spirit has been given many names: Helper, Comforter, Advocate, Strengthener, Counselor, and Intercessor, to name a few. Whatever you may choose to call Him, He provokes in me a deep love for the one who is my constant companion. He makes it possible for me to say, "Jesus in Me." He allows me to live my life with a higher purpose.

Important Observation - If you ride the fence of complacency, the enemy (Satan) will leave you alone. That is one of his biggest weapons, to keep you lukewarm. Trust me, there truly is a spiritual battle going on constantly as the enemy will try to pull you down with lies, half-truths, and discouragement. But, because you are pursuing God, desiring to learn how to love Him with all your heart, soul, mind, and strength, he will be after you to try to discredit in your mind all you will be learning in this book. He will cloud your thinking and bring all sorts of doubts and difficulties to light to dissuade you from believing the "Truth." Don't listen to him! Remember, Jesus has already won the victory, and He is *in* you!

> *Jesus has already won the victory, and He is in you!*

I encourage you to test all that is shared within these pages against Scripture to verify the truth. It is so important we know what the Bible says because Satan loves to bring to mind twisted half-truths. They may sound similar to Scripture we may have heard in the past, but he distorts it and can easily lead us astray if we don't know correctly what the Scriptures say. We are to live and die by this Book, so we need to know what it says. It will lead us to the heart of God.

To get back to the concept of holiness and perfection, I want to explain these because I think these two words can be very confusing as to what is expected from us as believers and may appear to be beyond reach. I want to minimize any stumbling blocks that might keep you from experiencing victory because of any feelings of inadequacy.

In God's Word, He commands us to be holy, perfect, and pure like Him and His Son, and He would not command something from us that was impossible or offer us something He was not willing or able to give (1 Peter 1:14–16, 1 John 2:1, 3:3,9, Hebrews 12:14).

As mentioned earlier, there is no way to achieve the victorious life on our own. But Jesus can make and keep us holy and give us victory. Paul encourages us in 1 Corinthians 15:57: "But thanks be to God, who gives us the victory through our Lord Jesus Christ."

Perfect Love
What is it and How Do We Live It?

Now, let me ease your concerns about what it means to be "perfect," as summarized throughout the New Testament. What do the two words "holiness" and "perfection" mean? Are they synonymous? As Christians, we see the command and aim at "holiness," but "perfection" just seems too "out of reach," yet it is a command. So what is perfection?

Christ said: "You, therefore, must be perfect as your Father is perfect" (Matthew 4:48), which seems to demand some sort of perfection in our lifetime. What is so perfect about God? In a word, *everything!* He is perfectly sinless and exhibits perfection in all kinds of incredible attributes *we* could never attain. He is God, and we are only human. He was referring back to the previous two verses (Matthew 5:46–47), making the point we are not to love only those who love us back or greet only our own kind; we are to love everyone.

So what is Jesus talking about here with "Perfect Love"—we are to love perfectly as God loves us. Isn't that what the whole redemption story is all about? Jesus came out of love—that's why He died for us. His love is perfect, and He showed us how to love perfectly. We are called to a perfect love, and that is the crux of living a victorious life.

As mentioned earlier, in Mark 12:30-31, when Jesus was asked what the most important commandment was, He said: "You shall love the Lord your God with all your heart and with all your soul and with all your mind and with all you strength. The second is this: 'You shall love your neighbor as yourself.' There is no other commandment greater than these."

When we can learn to love like that, we will be well on our way to experiencing a victorious life. When we love God and others perfectly, we will find everything else will fall into place.

As Jesus's ministry was coming to a close, He said in John 13:34-35, "A new commandment I give to you, that you love one another: just as I have loved you, you also are to love one another. By this all men will know that you are my disciples, if you love one another."

According to a search on the Blue Letter Bible, the word "love" is mentioned around two hundred times in the New Testament depending on the translation.[3] I will only name a few here, but we must look at what the Bible says about God's love and its possible effect on us as we experience Him living His life through us. First John 4:19 states: "We love because he first loved us."

Paul reminds us in Romans 13:10 love is what enables us to obey God—a crucial factor in experiencing the fullness of God, and therefore, a victorious Christian life. "Love does no wrong to a neighbor; therefore love is the fulfilling of the law."

We will spend the majority of this book unpacking what all is involved in this process of loving perfectly. Remember, this is a journey—a marathon—not a sprint. Be prepared for this to take time to sink in and even longer to live out.

When you accept Jesus's sacrifice on the cross for your salvation, that is instantaneous, but the sanctification process is precisely that—a process—a journey for the rest of your life. The joy is in the journey, so plan a lifetime of travel. Learn to enjoy the ride, even though there will inevitably be some bumps along the way. The satisfaction and peace you will gain from this experience will far outweigh the inconveniences.

We need to remember when we became a Christ-follower, we were crucified with Christ. The crucified life is one entirely given over to the Lord in absolute humility and obedience, which is described as a sacrifice pleasing to the Lord. What is humility? It is "others" centered, so has little to do with how we feel. Instead, it has a lot to do with our focus and how well we treat others.

His love compels us to radical obedience. He needs to be *everything* to us. We should strive to think like Him, act like Him, and love like Him. The crux of spiritual perfection has everything to do with Christ—not with rules or regulations. Colossians 3:14 tells us we are to "...put on love..."

If we want God's blessing, putting on love and depending absolutely on Him is the way to go. If that is true, and we are absolutely surrendered to Him, then we should be dead to our fleshly desires, and it should be Christ living His perfect life through us. Genuine love for God leads to wholehearted obedience.

> *Genuine love for God leads to wholehearted obedience.*

Let's think about that for a minute. If we are crucified, what does that mean? We are most certainly dead. We are dead to the control of our old life of habitual sin. When we died to self, we became alive in Christ, meaning He is alive in us and desires more than anything to live His life through us. This means we must consciously and intentionally submit (give up) control to Him in surrendering our old, bad habits. We can only do this through the power of the Holy Spirit, which now lives in us.

Romans 5:5 tells us: "...and hope does not put us to shame, because God's love has been poured into our hearts through the Holy Spirit who has been given to us."

I love what is called the "High Priestly Prayer" in John 17:6-26 when Jesus prays for His disciples. He is ultimately praying for all future believers when He prays this to the Father. He closes with this in verse 26: "I made known to them your name, and I will continue to make it known, that the love with which you have loved me may be in them, and I in them."

That is the only way we mortals can love perfectly. We have the power through the Spirit to love as God loves Jesus, and He loves us. What I get from this is perfect love is possible for us, but only when Jesus who personifies love dwells in our hearts. First John 4:12 tells us: "... if we love one another, God abides in us and his love is perfected in us."

Continuing in verses 16-17: "So we have come to know and to believe the love that God has for us. God is love, and whoever abides in love abides in God, and God abides in him. By this is love perfected with us, so that we may have confidence for the Day of Judgment, because as he is so also are we in this world."

Just as surely as God is Spirit, He is love, and love is not just something God does; it's who He is. God would have to stop *being* to stop *loving*. So while "love" is a verb, it's also a noun when it comes to God. God *IS* love. We know God takes up residence in our lives in the form of the Holy Spirit at the time of our conversion. With that comes the love of God into our hearts. That is how we love perfectly. He loves through us. That can only happen consistently if we are constantly surrendered to Him.

> *God would have to stop being to stop loving.*

I know I have thrown a lot at you in these many pages, but I would like to give you a real-life example of the power of our love for God. A friend of ours had fallen out of love with his wife. Divorce was not an option for him, and so he asked a friend to pray for him so that his love for his wife would return. His friend simply said, "Dude, you just need to love Jesus more."

He said, "What?"

His friend responded, "You heard me. You just need to love Jesus more, and then your love for your wife will return."

He was right! My friend followed his friend's advice, and miraculously it worked! He poured himself into God's Word and spent a lot of time in prayer and worship. His heart was transformed, and he fell in love with Jesus in a fresh new way. Along with that, he fell in love with his wife all over again. During the years since, they have a fantastic relationship—the envy of many of their friends.

When our vertical relationship with the Lord is intact and healthy, then and only then will our horizontal relationships be what they should be. Then you will experience a victorious life—the life you always wanted.

As for God's love for us, Paul encourages us in Ephesians 3:17-19, "So that Christ may dwell in your hearts through faith—that you, being rooted and grounded in love, may have strength to comprehend with all the saints what is the breadth and length and height and depth, and to know the love of Christ that surpasses knowledge, that you may be filled with all the fullness of God."

If we have the mind of Christ and the power from on high in us to fulfill His purposes, "holiness" becomes not just second nature, but also our very life.

We must remember Christ (in the form of the Holy Spirit) is already in the heart of every believer. But unless He has total possession and full control, we cannot have victory. In Luke 24:49, Jesus told us we would be "...clothed with power from on high." Paul, in 1 Corinthians 2:16, boldly says, "We have the mind of Christ." So, if we have the mind of Christ and the power from on high in us to fulfill His purposes, "holiness" becomes not just second nature, but also our very life.

If we indeed do have the mind and heart of Christ, we also have His disposition, which should show up in our countenance, as well as many of His attributes. The fruit of the Spirit (listed in Galatians 5:22–24) is an excellent example of much of His character.

When He "becomes" our life, then we have "experienced" Him and indeed "know" Him in the biblical sense. "And this is eternal life, that they know you, the only true God and Jesus Christ who you have sent" (John 17:3).

Jesus Christ is "perfect love," and perfect love casts out not only fear but all sin. You may still be asking, "How can I, a struggling sinner, though saved by grace, get this 'perfect love'? How can I get victory over all the known sins in my life, and live the victorious life?"

When we are aware of our sins, our first reaction usually is to fight our temptations. This is why we most often fail. It might work for a while if our willpower holds out, but fighting or struggling against temptation is not biblical. The Bible does not say we are to "fight temptation" but to "flee" from sin, youthful lusts, idolatry, and such.

James, in 4:7, tells us to resist the devil, and he will flee. First Peter 5:9 tells us to resist the devil, standing firm in the faith. We are to "stand," not "struggle." We are to live, stand, and walk by faith. According to Ephesians 6, the "shield of faith" can quench all the fiery darts of the evil one. Every dart Satan can fire at us can be extinguished by faith. It is by faith we can overcome the evil one. To fear is actually to have more confidence in your antagonist than in Christ. Faith trusts God is in control, and He can do it all. Faith believes what God has said to the point of acting on it whether or not we feel like it.

When He "becomes" our life, then we have "experienced" Him and indeed "know" Him in the biblical sense.

Jesus Christ has already won the victory for us. We just need to claim it. Satan and sin have been defeated. The only power it can now have is the power you give it. John reminds us in 1 John 4:4, "He who is in you is greater than he who is in the world." So we come back to the same theme: The secret of success is the indwelling Christ. This is the truth, and genuine life change always begins with the truth.

> *To fear is actually to have more confidence in your antagonist than in Christ.*

Victory is in *trusting,* not *trying:* "For everyone who has been born of God overcomes the world. And this is the victory that has overcome the world—our faith" (1 John 5:4). It is speaking here about overcoming our sin. Victory over sin is a gift from God through Jesus (1 Corinthians 15:57).

The gift itself is instantaneous and perfect, not gradual. It's the process of letting that gift permeate our heart that takes time. Sin is sin, and all sins have their root in the heart. For the believer who has had a "heart change," habitual sin has been conquered by Christ once and for all. As far as our occasional sin goes, all we can do is confess it, look to Christ in faith, and let Him overcome it for us.

God's gifts are perfect. He gave us Jesus Christ Himself to dwell in our hearts in the form of the Holy Spirit to help us to live by faith following His will.

First John 5:18 tells us: "We know that everyone who has been born of God does not keep on sinning, but he who was born of God protects him, and the evil one does not touch him."

> *Victory is in trusting, not trying.*

Can you believe that and trust Christ to do it in you? If you have trouble accepting any facts I share with you in this book, just ask the Holy Spirit to help you with your unbelief. He will reveal the truth to you.

God alone has unfailing love and desires more than we can know to flood us with it. To live a victorious life, we must learn to pour out our hearts to God, confessing our sin daily

71

so nothing will hinder His ability to live and love through us. There is nothing more satisfying than to know you are living in the center of God's will, being used of Him to love perfectly.

SURRENDER
WHAT IS IT, AND WHAT DO WE NEED TO DO?

To go back to our verse about loving God with all our heart, soul, mind, and strength, we actively love God with all our *hearts* when we surrender to Him and His authority, knowing how much He loves us. Only He deserves our ultimate love and longs for our desires to be as properly ordered as His own. We love Him with our *soul* and *mind* when we daily decide to surrender the innermost places of our thought lives to Him asking Him to take control of that area. We love Him with all our *strength* when we give Him all we have, whether it be little or a lot.

> *The secret of success is the indwelling Christ.*

I would never say surrender is easy. I know—I've been struggling with it in some areas for a long time, and I know my journey is far from over. It's not for the faint of heart who are indulged and pampered. Your old self will whimper and fight for survival, but the reward is *so* worth it. Surrender results in rewards we would never otherwise experience, and the bigger the struggle to surrender, the grander the rewards. To quote John the Baptist, speaking of Jesus: "He must increase, but I must decrease" (John 3:30).

For this to happen, I must Surrender *All*.

Why did Jesus go through all He did on the cross? Hebrews 12:2 says Jesus went to the cross "...for the joy that was set before him..."

First, He loved us so much, and He wanted what God most wanted and hated what God most hated. He trusted God and knew the end of the story. Can you trust God for His promises? We can only be on board if God is prominent in our hearts. This is how Jesus was one with God. He only did what God wanted Him to do. Jesus always knew God's will, and He did it. He could do God's will because He knew God's heart. The Holy Spirit (Christ in us) gives us that same ability.

How can we get this indwelling of Christ? How can we know we have Him and thus "know Him and the power of His resurrection," as quoted by Paul in Philippians 3:10? Brother Lawrence experienced an amazingly victorious life as he explains in his book, *The Practice of the Presence of God*.[4] He was a devoted monk living in the 1600s in Paris, France. In this little booklet, he explained he learned how to stay in constant connection with God through ongoing prayer as he would envision God being with him every moment of every day. He was able to put into practice the Scripture: "Pray without ceasing" (1 Thessalonians 5:17). If we stay alert in prayer, Jesus will share His heart with us. If we are open and willing to go deep with Him, we can experience His inmost thoughts.

On the contrary, when we take our eyes off Jesus, we can be easily distracted. It's so common for us to get busy and bogged down with work and activities that we can simply forget God is in us in the person of the Holy Spirit. He is ready, willing, and able to give us divine guidance, direction, and wisdom every moment of every day. Somehow Brother Lawrence had mastered that.

I have certainly been guilty of letting life get in the way! I can't tell you how many mornings I have jumped out of bed and hit the floor running, knowing it would be a hectic day, and I had better just get started. As I look back on those days, I can see I spent a lot of time "spinning my wheels." I didn't mean to leave God out. I just didn't give

Him the time of day. When I would realize what I had done, I would have to pray and ask God to forgive me for my self-sufficiency. When we find ourselves getting "stuck," it's usually because we have been seeking our way rather than seeking God's face.

Brother Lawrence learned how to experience the constant presence of God through incessant prayer mentally. He surrendered himself entirely to God. Without such surrender, one cannot practice the continual presence of God. He states in his book, the heart must be empty of all other things, because, "God will possess the heart alone."[2] It must be devoid of anything else. It must be empty so that He can fill it with Himself. Only if it is vacant, can He do what He pleases. He must have all of us every day all day. Isn't that what we want in pursuit of the victorious life? The more we practice His presence, the more we experience His presence, and the more mature we will become.

We need to realize one does not fully appropriate a victorious life merely by accepting Christ as our Savior from the guilt of sin. Many sincere Christians, unfortunately, are still living defeated lives. Their sinful passions and desires are not entirely gone. There are failures, and their lives end up not looking much different from those of the world.

There must be a complete surrender of self—a yearning desire to be free from all known sin. We must look to Jesus Christ by faith to destroy *all* the sin in us and invite Christ to be our whole life—literally to *be* our life. We will *never* experience the victorious life unless Jesus Christ has all there is of us—*Never!*

> *We will never experience the victorious life unless Jesus Christ has all there is of us—Never!*

There are two parts to surrender. One is absolute surrender of our will to what God wants *us* to do, and the other is to surrender to allow God to work in us to do His good pleasure.

If He comes and takes the entire possession of your total being, He will allow you to experience the victorious Christian life, and you can honestly say, "I live, and yet no longer I, but Christ lives in me." When He possesses you wholly, then you shall be holy. Are you willing to release the grip on your life and relinquish yourself unreservedly into His hands? Have you made, or are you ready to make Him not just Savior, but Lord? To do so is to secure heaven right now—on earth.

Review:

So let's review for a minute. Our goal is to become like Christ, right? The reason? So we can glorify God with our lives, and so others will be drawn to Him. The purpose of the Holy Spirit? To see that Christ is fashioned within us to reveal Christ in us. We receive the Holy Spirit automatically when we become a believer—a Christ-follower, but He will only inhabit what we relinquish to Him. If there are any areas of our life we are unwilling to surrender, we are sadly hampering our ability to have the most intimate relationship with Christ.

Do you struggle with obedience? If you ask God to give you the desire to remain obedient continually, He will. He will help you to want to obey Him and will provide you with His power to do so. You will begin to long to hear from Him every day as you better understand His character and His heart as you seek to be more like Him. You will discover how deep the Father's love is for you, which will give you a feeling of acceptance and significance you would not get any other way. We must forsake all else to follow Christ and allow Him to take possession of our heart.

It is so easy to quench or grieve the Holy Spirit when we withhold from Him or ignore His warnings. So He might be present but could very well be dormant. It is up to us to continually pray for Him to fill us daily and be willing to let Him lead. When we do, not only will He fill us, and we will be wonderfully conscious of the indwelling Christ, but others will see Him in us as well. Our whole countenance will change to reflect the love of Christ when the Holy Spirit is active in our lives.

Be careful about resisting the Holy Spirit's leading in your life, especially if He is trying to convict you of sin. You may not like what He is directing to do, but His words will guide and direct you to abundant life. If you ignore Him often enough, He will quit trying to get your attention, which could result in a hardened heart.

I must emphasize "we" cannot overcome any sin or gain His grace by "trying." Christ has already extended His grace to us and conquered sin for us. We don't have to do what He has already done. He *does* ask us to enter into His victory by accepting what He has done and resting in Him. We are reminded in Colossians 1:27: "...Christ in you the hope of glory."

Other religions try their best to work their way to God to earn His favor, but the true God of the universe came down to meet us where we are. Jesus came and lived as a man. He was fully God and fully man— Emmanuel, "God with us!" Isn't it incredible the Creator of the Universe, who inhabits eternity, whose name is Holy among many other marvelous names, not only dwells on High but also in our hearts?

We already talked a bit about the mighty power of the Holy Spirit. If even a little of our surrender is withdrawn or withheld, we will experience diminished power. But if we gladly submit fully to our blessed Master, He (the Holy Spirit) will come and fill us with His divine presence. If we trust our *all* to Him, He will become "all in all" to us. Are you "All In?"

WHAT IS THE VICTORIOUS LIFE AND HOW DO WE LIVE IT?

DIVING DEEPER

1. In summary, what are the key points of this chapter? What does the victorious Christian life look like?

2. Do you struggle with obedience and surrender? What does that look like to you? What can you do this week to turn that around?

3. What does it mean to "Practice the presence of Christ?" What can you do to cultivate that habit?

4. What picture comes to mind when you think of the word "holy?" Do you think of it as a positive quality, negative, or just neutral? Can you expand on your answer?

5. According to the author, our primary goal as a Christ-follower is to be Christ-like. What does that look like? How do we attain that? What would be the benefits, the drawbacks?

6. Which verse(s) were the most impactful to you in this chapter, and why?

7. How does your thinking/behavior line up with the content of this chapter?

8. What obstacles do you see could hinder you from living a victorious life?

9. What is one fundamental truth from this chapter you sense the Spirit is urging you to embrace?

10. What changes would you like to apply in your life?

Chapter 5

What Does Total Surrender Look Like?

Surrender—this is a hard word and concept for many. Believe me, when God is involved, it is for our good. Let me try to explain. So far, besides "perfect love" and "holiness," we have talked about the importance of two things to experience the "victorious" life—*"surrender/obedience"* and *"faith"*—our part as well as God's part. God wants us to desire Him above all else, and the love of Christ compels us to choose total obedience. We have already alluded to it in previous chapters, but let's dig in, so we really understand the importance and impact of it in our lives.

When we surrender our lives/heart to God, and He comes to live inside us in the person of the Holy Spirit, we have the power to experience lasting hope and pure joy regardless of our circumstances. Joy should be a defining characteristic of who we are.

> *Joy should be a defining characteristic of who we are.*

The words "surrender" and "give up" are not popular words and often have a negative connotation. However, when we get to the end of our rope and realize we cannot power through our struggles on our own and we "give them up" or "surrender" them up to Christ, that's when we can experience the fullness of God's love, guidance, and wisdom. It's when we learn to trust and rest in Him we experience peace. It's when we "give up" we "gain." It's surrender to God that brings complete life.

LIVING THE LIFE YOU ALWAYS WANTED

It's when we "give up" we "gain."

We can always tell in whom or what we put our trust because that is where we go first. Why is it we so often wait until we are at the end of our resources before we turn to the Lord with our struggles as a last resort? As you experience more and more of the victorious life, going to Him first will become a *way* of life. It's not our nature, so it must be intentional until it becomes natural.

First, we must be willing to give up all known sin, our self-will, and our selfishness and willingly surrender it all into God's hands. Then in faith, we must look to God to continue to pursue our hearts to sanctify us. Remember, this is a journey, and we must learn to "let go and let God." That includes things in the past that are forgiven, but possibly not yet relinquished. Are you perhaps being held back from surrendering to Christ because you feel too unworthy? Realize your worthiness is not dependent on you or anything you have done; it is in Christ.

What God wants from us is not our goodness or efforts to do better. He just wants our sins. That is all He wants from us in exchange for His righteousness. We must surrender all pretense we are anything, give up all claims of even being worthy of Him. Once we do that, the Holy Spirit will show each of us individually what we need to surrender next.

During this process, we have to give up claims to any rights. When we begin to see ourselves as the Lord sees us, it's not our sins so much that shock us as the awful nature of pride that surfaces, which we did not even know was so strong. When we see ourselves as the Lord does, the shame, horror, and desperate conviction hit home. We're challenged to live with God in no other way other than His way, identifying with Him in His death. True surrender means absolute devotion to Him. Showing no concern for the uncertainties in the world is the secret of walking with Jesus.

"Let go and let God."

What Does Total Surrender Look Like?

Christ came to take us into Himself, and He comes into us. He is the head, and we are His body. He is the Vine, and we are the branches, as explained in John 15:1-11. We need to make sure we stay connected to Him because apart from Him, we can do nothing. It is *only* through our connection with Him that we can experience the abundant, victorious life He offers.

Let's talk about the vine for a minute and its relationship to the branches. It is such a great metaphor of the Christian life. What's it like to be a branch? For one thing, it is dependent on the vine for nourishment. The vine does all the work, and the branch merely receives what it needs from the vine to grow the grapes. The branch is entirely dependent on the vine. That is significant. The power to the branches cannot be sporadic. It is a vital relationship that has to be continual and healthy.

> *True surrender means absolute devotion to Him.*

The branch in the vine represents our place as a servant. We must daily be conscious of the importance of abiding in Christ, realizing without the Vine we are nothing. Think about the word "nothing," If we are "something," then God cannot be "everything." We must become "nothing."[1] Besides the branch being entirely dependent, a branch is at rest. If we are to be an actual branch of Christ, who is the living Vine, we also need to rest in Him and let Him carry the responsibility. We cannot produce heavenly fruit unless we are in a vital relationship with Christ, the Vine. Our mission is to "abide in the vine," allowing God to do through us what only He can do. We must remember He is God, and we are not.

One more thing to tie all this together—the sap of the Heavenly Vine is the Holy Spirit. He gives it life. To bear fruit, what we desperately must receive from Christ is nothing less than a strong inflowing of the Holy

Spirit. The more we abide in the Vine, the more fruit we will bear. We are to live an abiding life.[2]

God wants nothing more than for us to abide in Him. While the "doing" is important, He would much rather we spend more time "being"—resting in Him. Imagine curling up in His lap every morning with His arms wrapped around you as you talk to Him, praising Him for who He is, soaking up His love, and getting your daily assignment from His Word and promptings from the Holy Spirit. It doesn't get any better than that.

I love to watch baptisms because, as the person goes under the water, it reminds me of how, when we give our lives to Christ, our old life dies, and we are buried with Him (unto His death). If you think about it, sin cannot have dominion over a dead person. How cool is that! Then, when the person baptized is raised out of the water, it reminds me of being made alive in Christ as a new creation, as in His resurrection.

While baptism saves no one, it is an outward expression and reminder of the lifelong personal commitment of living out the heart/life change brought on by God's saving grace. First, we die to self; then Christ becomes our life. Sometimes we just have to get out of the way. John 12:24 tells us, "unless a grain of wheat falls into the earth and dies, it remains alone, but if it dies, it bears much fruit."

> *The more we abide in the Vine, the more fruit we will bear.*

Death is necessary for life. We cannot experience His resurrection power in our life if we have not died with Him first. He cannot fill what we have not emptied. If we are holding onto "Stuff," there is no room for Him.

We should have the same attitude as Paul, as stated in Philippians 3:8. He certainly understood the benefit of knowing Christ: "Indeed, I count everything as loss because of the surpassing worth of knowing Christ Jesus my Lord. For his sake I have suffered the loss of all things and count them as rubbish, in order that I may gain Christ."

When we claim forgiveness of our sins, we also, with God's help, renounce the influences of this world as we look to God in faith to raise us to walk in the newness of life. Let's take a good look at what death and resurrection meant to our Lord. There He was—perfect God and perfect man nailed to the cross. There He bore the weight of all the sins of the world. God Himself cannot die, nor can He even look upon sin, so the Spirit of God in the perfect man—Jesus, abandoned that body of clay. He "yielded up His spirit."

> *He cannot fill what we have not emptied.*

There a dead man hangs upon the cross. That perfect body is then buried, and on the third day, God raised Him from the dead. What does that mean? The Spirit of Christ came back into that dead fleshly body, and Jesus Christ rose again—once more perfect God and perfect man.

God wants the same for all of us. We can genuinely believe Romans 6:4-11, which says:

> ...so we too might walk in newness of life. For if we have been united with him in a death like His, we shall certainly be united with him in a resurrection like His. We know that our old self was crucified with him in order that the body of sin might be brought to nothing so that we would no longer be enslaved to sin. For one who has died has been set free from sin. Now if we have died with Christ, we believe that we will also live with him. We know that Christ, being raised from the dead, will never

die again; death no longer has dominion over him. For the death he died he died to sin, once for all, but the life he lives he lives to God. So you also must consider yourselves dead to sin and alive to God in Christ Jesus.

When we identify with Christ in His death and resurrection, then "our life" is no longer ours but is the "Christ-life"—*not* an imitation of Christ, but Christ Himself dwelling in our hearts by faith. Then we can humbly say with Paul: "I have been crucified with Christ. It is no longer I who live, but Christ who lives in me. And the life I now live in the flesh I live by faith in the Son of God, who loved me and gave himself for me" (Galatians 2:20). What an incredible privilege and responsibility at the same time. Are you willing to do this?

I won't lie to you. Living the crucified life in a fallen world is not easy by any means. You may find it is one of the most challenging things you have ever done. The cost can be very high, and the path can sometimes be lonely and quite rough. However, the reward of having such an intimate relationship with Christ through it all will be well worth the journey.

When I was in college, I remember struggling with doing God's will. Oh, how I wanted to but knew I often failed. My new prayer became, "Lord, make me 'willing to be willing' to do whatever is necessary to carry out your will." Maybe you need to ask God to make you "willing to be willing" to "surrender all" to His Lordship. "All" is the all-important word.

Do you remember the ancient story in Greek mythology about the goddess who wanted to make her son Achilles immortal? She dipped him under the waters of the River Styx which would make him impenetrable like armor. The only thing is, she held him by the ankle, so his heel was left vulnerable, and that is where he became mortally wounded. There is a moral to this story.

Satan knows where we are vulnerable. He knows if he can just get to us at one weak spot, he can take us down. Even though our salvation is secure, he knows if he can just prevent us from "full surrender," he can prevent us from experiencing a victorious life while on this earth. This intervention also allows him to hinder our positive influence in the world.

Instead of worrying about what God might expect or require of us if we surrender, we need to remember what Jesus said in John 15:11, "These things I have spoken to you, that my joy may be in you, and that your joy may be full."

He said this right after He talked about abiding in Him and keeping His commandments. Of course, if He dwells in us and lives His life in us, we experience the very joy of God! We are to "rejoice evermore!"

So often, we run from God to escape retribution, but what we are doing is avoiding His rescue. He knows everything about us—past, present, and future—and even our thoughts. How amazing to think we can or would even want to hide anything from Him when He always wants what's best for us and to bless us out of His abundant everlasting, unconditional love.

I have a question for you. If you had a child who climbed up into your lap and said,

"Mommy/Daddy, I love you so much. From now on, I will do whatever you ask me to do without even asking why." After falling over in total shock, would you think to yourself, "Wow, now that I have that kind of cooperation, what could I do to make this child miserable?" Of course not! You would vow in your heart to do everything you could to nurture that sweet spirit.

Will our God of love take advantage of us if we surrender all to Him? Remember, He has not only the power but the will to make us extremely happy. As our future plans go, does He not know what is best for us? Yet we are often unwilling to trust Him to give us His best. We must yield our whole life over to Jesus, so we can identify with His death, becoming nothing in ourselves, and then receiving the life of Christ and the power of the Holy Spirit to do all and be all for us. He wants to be our "all in all."

He may even bring us far more good than we ever expected. He is our God, who is willing and able to do far above all we could ever ask or think (See Ephesians 3:20). Once we understand and can accept there is no greater love than God's, then we will be ready to take the first step toward surrender and experience the victorious life.

Looking at Christ as our example, He received His life from God and lived it in dependence on Him, also yielding His life to God through complete obedience. Obedience is the surrendering of our will to the will of another. When Jesus surrendered His life to God, He taught us the only thing worth living for is a life submitted to God, even unto death. If we insist on controlling our life and spending it on ourselves, even partly, we are abusing it and taking it away from God's original purpose. We need to learn from Christ the beauty and purpose of having life so we can surrender it to God and then allow Him to fill it with His glory.

We should live today for what matters tomorrow. God only gives grace when we need it—not ahead of time.

As far as our present situation goes, we need to consistently take inventory to see if there is anyone with whom we are withholding love. Is there any situation or person causing bitterness, irritability, pride, jealousy, resentment, or anything negative that we need to address? If so, you are robbing yourself from experiencing the victorious life. Give it to Jesus, and He will kill it. Remember, no one "makes" you mad. Sure, someone may aggravate you to no end, but how you respond or react is your responsibility.

Keep in mind the past is the past. While we might (hopefully) learn from it, we must not dwell on it or get stuck there. We need to let it go. Also, while we need to plan for the future, we need to plan for now, and "now" is the present. We need not be anxious about it. Be careful not to allow any fear of the future rob you of present victory. First Peter 5:7 reminds us to cast all our anxiety on Christ because He cares for us.

While it's good to plan for the future, we need to live in the present. Rather than focusing our thoughts too much on future plans, remember to live in the present enough to experience the victory of Christ in the moment. We should live today for what matters tomorrow. God only gives grace when we need it—not ahead of time. Don't miss it by not seizing the day.

We must be careful to remember surrender is not merely promising God to give up sin and always to do His will. Instead, it is turning over to God all we are and all we have for Him to do with us whatever He wishes.

Unfortunately, many so-called "surrendered" Christians often feel defeated because they misunderstand and think they can carry out their good intentions with God's help—having God join them to help them carry out their will. No! When we surrender to Jesus, it is not just an act to receive Him as Savior with the expectation He will help us in our time of trouble. He becomes our Master, and we are to forsake *all* to follow Him. We have the privilege and opportunity to join *Him* in what *He* is doing.

God simply requires us to be faithful in our obedience to carry out His orders. God has a plan, and we often are required to "wait" for our marching orders. To wait on God is our highest and most important work. The Holy Spirit comes in response to "believing" prayer. Prayer is so essential I have devoted a whole chapter to it. Too often, we make our plans thinking we know what to do, asking God to bless our efforts instead of first asking God to go before us and waiting for His direction.

Obedience to Christ's commands always brings fulfillment. On occasion, He may ask us to do things that may not make total sense until long after we have completed them. He often won't reveal the details or reason for the mission—just enough to carry through His assignment, so we depend on Him and His guidance. Our response will determine what He does next in our life.

What we do in God's will has His strength behind it as well as His blessing. So our first desire should be to have the will of God revealed. Caution: God will only reveal His will to a humble, surrendered, tender, and quiet heart. He desires us to be surrendered to the Holy Spirit, having full dominion over every area of our life. That is not something that comes naturally. For this to happen, this partnership and submission to the Holy Spirit must become intentional, conscious action.

We are to turn ourselves over to God, let Him take possession of our heart, and then trust Christ to do His part. He is able! It's not our surrender that gives us the victory; it's not even our faith. While both are essential, it is Christ Himself, the faithful One who will never fail you! We experience the most amazing blessings when we allow the Holy Spirit to direct our Christian work, which is in response to our obedience to Him.

What Does Total Surrender Look Like?

When we surrender ourselves to God, we exchange or give up our thoughts, feelings, and desires for new ones—for His. He must have all of us every day all day. We can only do this through faith. Then we can believe God is who He says He is, and He will do exactly what He promised. If He gives you a promise, you can count on Him fulfilling it in His perfect manner and timing. Our lives become a reflection of His presence and love, not a list of our human accomplishments. We only truly experience fulfillment when we submit ourselves to God and give ourselves entirely to Him. Then we can allow Him to use us to be examples of His love and forgiveness and, by so doing, draw others to Him.

He would never command anything of you He would not enable you to do.

Do you know the story in the gospels about the woman who had been hemorrhaging incurably for twelve years, and no physician could help her? Culturally, she was considered ceremonially unclean because of her bleeding. She was impoverished, lonely, and almost hopeless. I say "almost" because, on this particular day, she heard Jesus, the great healer, would be in town. She believed if she could just touch the edge of His garment, she would be healed. Breaking every rule and social norm, she pushed through the crowd and got to Him. Immediately, she was healed.

When Jesus felt the power drain from Him, He turned around and asked who touched Him. With fear and trembling, she spoke up and shared her story. His response? "Daughter, your faith has made you well; go in peace, and be healed of your disease" (Mark 5:34).

In an instant, she was no longer a "bleeding" woman, but a highly treasured daughter of the King. That is the only place in Scripture where Jesus calls a woman "daughter." How special is that? All because of her surrender and faith in Him.

To experience God's radical, abundant, and unexpected blessings, we need to be sure we release our grip on what we think we love and want. We must offer our full obedience and absolute surrender as we yield to Him, saying, "The answer is yes, Lord, now what is the question? What is it You want me to do?" Again, we know His plan is perfect, right? How could we want anything else? To have the opportunity and privilege to be a part of that is extraordinary!

As a Christ-follower, our relationship with Christ is like that of a servant to his master. Since Jesus bought us with His blood, we must choose to follow Him and live every day with the thought, "How can I please my Master?" As mentioned earlier, there is no other relationship as important as the one we have with our Creator. Any other relationships are secondary.

The secret of the spiritual life is to learn to say, "I surrender everything." The absolute surrender of everything into God's hands is necessary. If our hearts are willing to do that, there's no limit to what God will do for us or the blessings He will pour out. The condition for experiencing the fullness of God's grace and blessings is absolute surrender to Him.

If you have any fear of surrendering, realize God can make you willing. Just ask Him. He would never command anything of you He would not enable you to do. Your desire for Him in your heart is a result of His working in you. He who lived a life of absolute surrender is residing in your heart in the person of His Holy Spirit. You may have hindered Him in the past, but He is committed to helping you find the place of full surrender through your humility and waiting upon Him. God always accepts our act of submission to Him, and He wants to bless you!

WHAT DOES TOTAL SURRENDER LOOK LIKE?

When you allow Jesus to rewire your heart and change the focus of your affections and desires off yourself and embrace His, there is no telling how He can use you. To be surrendered to God is of more value even than your personal holiness. Once you are totally surrendered to Him, He will work through you all the time. You won't even realize it because He will so consume you, and it will become second nature. There is *nothing* more rewarding than knowing you are fully surrendered—in the center of God's will, living and serving the risen Christ, using your experiences good and bad to develop your character to match your calling.

Diving Deeper

1. What does it mean to be totally surrendered? What do we have to give up?

2. Why is it we tend to fight total surrender? Why is trusting God such a struggle?

3. Do you struggle with surrendering control of your life (or a certain area of your life) over to God? In what ways? What steps can you take to relinquish control?

4. Summarize the metaphor of the Vine and the branches and how it relates to the Christian life.

5. How do baptisms relate to our new life in Christ? Explain its relationship with death and resurrection (new life).

6. What happens when we are "crucified with Christ?"

7. Since Satan knows our salvation is secure and he cannot take it away, why does he bother harassing us?

8. What do we need to do as our part in achieving victory in this life? Explain.

9. How does your thinking/behavior line up with the content of this chapter?

10. What verse(s) spoke to you the most? Why? What main points/takeaways from this chapter do you feel the Holy Spirit would like for you to learn and embrace? How do you plan to respond?

Chapter 6

The Impact of Forgiveness

So far, I have not gone into detail about particular sins, but I feel one sin must be addressed. It is so important to understand the magnitude and devastation of unforgiveness.

If you have difficulty forgiving someone, you need to remember what Christ did for you on the cross. If He can forgive us for all our sins (past, present, and future), which He has, we can certainly forgive someone who has wronged us. Think about that. If you are a Christ-follower and have accepted the death of Jesus on your behalf, saving you from endless destruction forever and giving you eternal life in heaven—forgiving all your sins, you *must* pay it forward to those who have sinned against you. It doesn't matter how much someone may have hurt you.

> *If you have difficulty forgiving someone, you need to remember what Christ did for you on the cross.*

Besides God being "love," His nature is forgiveness. As Christ-followers, we *must* follow His example. If we insist on withholding forgiveness from anyone, our worship and prayers are futile. We must ask God to reveal areas where we are harboring resentment. We need to ask God to make us like Christ, so even during persecution, we can say, "Father, forgive them."

In Scripture, Jesus told us we can expect forgiveness from God as we forgive those who sin against us. He will forgive in the same way we forgive others (Matthew 6:15). This declaration does not suggest God will take away the salvation/justification from those who have already received the free pardon which He extends to all believers. Forgiveness, in that sense—a permanent and complete acquittal from the guilt and ultimate penalty of sin—belongs to all who are in Christ. However, Scripture also teaches God disciplines His children who disobey Him, and a lack of forgiveness on our part is a sin that will rob us of intimacy with Him.

> *Jesus never said certain offenses are unworthy of our forgiveness.*

We, as believers, are to continually confess our sins to receive a daily cleansing. This sort of forgiveness is simply a washing from the worldly violations of sin, not a repeat of the extensive cleansing from sin's corruption that comes with justification. It's like comparing a foot washing to a full bath. When we refuse to forgive, that is what God threatens to deny Christians who refuse to forgive others.

Jesus never said certain offenses are unworthy of our forgiveness. We have no biblical excuse for allowing any unforgiveness in our hearts. No offense committed against us is so heinous God's love cannot enable us to forgive. Forgiveness is not in any way a spiritual gift, a skill, or an inherited ability. It's a choice—an act of the will and is not a feeling. If we waited until we felt like forgiving anyone, we never would.

WHAT IS FORGIVENESS?

It's releasing another from the penalty of sin, so hopefully, the relationship can be restored. Depending on the other party, the restoration of the relationship is not always possible, but it should be our goal. It's canceling a debt owed to you and giving up any right for retribution. I know you may not feel like it and think a particular individual doesn't deserve to be forgiven, particularly if they have not even asked for it. That's okay. We certainly didn't deserve God's forgiveness, yet He forgave us anyway.

> *Forgiveness is a choice—an act of the will and is not a feeling.*

Forgiveness has little advantage to the one who caused pain. It mainly benefits you, the one who has been hurt. In reality, it is a gift you give to yourself. Otherwise, the bitterness of unforgiveness will eat away and probably even spill over into your other relationships. A spirit of unforgiveness is toxic.

Jesus commands us to forgive as an act of obedience, and when we do, the feelings will follow—maybe not right away, but they will eventually if you have genuinely forgiven and turned the results over to God. Forgiveness is a "one-time" event, but it is also an ongoing process of mentally letting it go. If this person deserves God's wrath, that's His business. Let Him deal with this person in His way. When someone offends us, our responsibility is to respond with forgiveness (Matthew 5:44). The real test of forgiveness is the ability to pray for God's blessing of the person we have forgiven.

You can be sure God will take the responsibility to see that justice is done. He loves people too much to allow sin to go unchecked. God is "just," which is all part of being "love." He alone can be sure justice is carried out appropriately.

Only by trusting in God's sovereign wisdom can we become free from our anger and preoccupation toward those who have committed sins against us or others. If we refuse to trust Him in this, it's easy to become enslaved to bitterness and anger. We must guard our hearts, trusting God to exercise His judgment against those needing chastening.

> *We need to realize our words judge us because they reveal the condition of our hearts.*

Few things are more destructive to Christians than anger. It causes us to lose self-control and say and do things we later regret. If not controlled, it turns to a bitterness that eats away at our hearts. We may end up giving the greatest speech we will ever regret. We need to realize our words judge us because they reveal the condition of our hearts.

When we hold on to bitter feelings toward someone, we are only hurting ourselves and our relationship with God. It's like drinking poison, hoping the other person will die. Forgiveness is removing the control the offender has over you. When we hang onto something that has happened to us in the past, it is just a memory. Why is it so often we try to keep it alive? What we focus on only makes it stronger.

As Pastor Andy Stanley states, "The one who benefits the most from forgiveness is the one who grants it, not the one who receives it."[1] We cannot have an intimate relationship with the Father or experience a victorious Christian life when we hold a grudge against our brother, spouse, neighbor, or whomever.

Do you need to ask someone for forgiveness? That's another thing we need to address to experience an abundant life. It's rather challenging to sense victory in your life if you know someone has bad feelings toward you whether or not you feel you deserve it. We are to be peacemakers. Paul admonishes us in Romans 12:18: "If possible, so far as it depends on you, live peaceably with all."

> *What we focus on only makes it stronger.*

The Impact of Forgiveness

True forgiveness is wanting the best for the offender and seeking reconciliation if possible. At least be faithful to do your best to bring closure of any unresolved issues in your life. If someone asks you for forgiveness, you *must* grant it. As difficult as all this might be, if you are obedient in asking for and granting forgiveness, there is a freedom that leads to experiencing a victorious life. Paul tells us in Colossians 3:13, "...if one has a complaint against another, forgiving each other; as the Lord has forgiven you, so you also must forgive."

> *"The one who benefits the most from forgiveness is the one who grants it, not the one who receives it."*

Jesus did not include an exemption clause for our reconciliation. Jesus tells us in Matthew 5:24 if someone has something against us, we are commanded to "be reconciled." God isn't interested in how "right" we are, but how "obedient" we are. Jesus calls for reconciliation to be sought eagerly, aggressively, and quickly even if it requires self-sacrifice. It's better to be wronged than to allow a dispute between believers to persist and thereby compromise a positive witness and dishonor Christ. God certainly knows what is going on, and your obedience will bless you.

God's command is not that we are always right and win arguments, but we are to respond with kindness and forgiveness when we are ill-treated. We bring Him no glory when winning a disagreement in His name. Still, we have an opportunity to reflect a Christ-like character when we demonstrate patience to those who mistreat us or misunderstand our motives. Arguing may never win others over to your view, but loving them as Christ does will win over many in time.

> *God isn't interested in how "right" we are, but how "obedient" we are.*

Do *you* need forgiveness from God right now for anything? It is so crucial for us to own our personal sin.

Brokenness is where we meet God, and if we genuinely want Him to use us, we often might need to be broken first. While it may be difficult at the time, it may be the best thing ever to happen to you. Then you can be used by God in surprising ways.

Maybe you need to ask God, as stated in Psalm 139:23-24: "Search me, O God, and know my heart! Try me and know my thoughts! And see if there be any grievous way in me, and lead me in the way everlasting!" First John 1:9 tells us: "If we confess our sins, he is faithful and just to forgive us our sins and to cleanse us from all unrighteousness."

When we fail, that does not weaken Christ. He has not failed, nor will He fail us. Once we forgive and are forgiven, we should not look back, but move on, turning our thoughts and focus toward the future. We can be thankful our past is forgiven, and as far as God is concerned, forgotten. Psalm 103:12 tells us, "as far as the east is from the west, so far does he remove our transgressions from us."

Remember Paul's comment in Philippians 3:13-14, "...forgetting what lies behind and straining forward to what lies ahead, I press on toward the goal for the prize of the upward call of God in Christ Jesus." We should make that our mantra as well. We cannot forget our past as God can, but we can let go of it and leave it in God's hands and move on.

My Story

I have a personal story about forgiveness and the freedom it brings. Hopefully, it can help you better understand the relationship between the two.

When I was twelve years old, my dad did things with me no father should do with his daughter. I was just going through puberty and was very confused at the time. He told me he was preparing me for marriage. Of course, my mom was not at home when these things were going on. I knew enough to know anything done in secret like that was wrong. I knew this was not normal, and it was probably not happening in other homes.

My dad was not forceful, as that was *not* his nature. I was compliant, as that *was* my nature. This behavior went on for quite a while until he got orders for Vietnam and went away for a year. I just made sure when he got back, I was never alone with him in a situation where it could happen again.

So, where does a young girl go to tell of such things? I didn't even consider it because, for one thing, I knew it would destroy my mom if she knew because she adored my dad, and I was afraid it could possibly end their marriage. If I told, he would probably lose his job, since he was a chaplain in the army. So I kept it a secret for many years.

As a young adult, I fantasized about confronting him to ask, "What was that all about." But I never had the courage until finally one day when he and my mom were visiting us. He went out to his car to get something, and I followed him out and asked him if we could sit in the car for a minute because I had a question for him. With fear and trembling, I asked him, "So...what was that about thirty years ago?" Without saying another word, he knew exactly what I was talking about and said, "That wasn't your fault."

I'm thinking, "Duh, I know that."

Then he said, "At least no harm was done."

I could only think, "Why in the world did I even bring this up?" I was so hoping he would say he was sorry and ask for my forgiveness. I wanted so much to be able to say I forgave him and felt I needed his apology for closure.

I don't know why I expected that. My dad was the type that even though he was a wonderful man in many ways, he was "never wrong," and so he never needed to apologize for anything, or ask for forgiveness. If he were ever exposed to be wrong about anything, he would just shrug his shoulders, laugh and say, "Oops, first mistake I ever made." So, by saying it wasn't my fault, I guess he was taking responsibility, and that was the closest I would get for an apology.

> *We cannot forget our past as God can, but we can let go of it and leave it in God's hands and move on.*

Needless to say, because he felt like "no harm was done," I felt worse than before I ever confronted him. I felt like I needed his apology for closure so I could tell him I forgave him. I knew it was vital for me to forgive my dad, and I wanted to, and even though I thought I had, I couldn't forget it and still got emotional when I thought about it.

So, I was afraid maybe I hadn't fully forgiven him. This really wore on me. It's not that I would dwell on it, but if I heard someone else share a similar story, the memories would come back, flooding my mind. So, I was afraid I hadn't actually forgiven him. That worried me because I knew how important it was to forgive him. I loved Jesus so much and wanted a close relationship with Him, but was afraid if I hadn't fully forgiven my dad, then that would keep me from having a close relationship with God.

I didn't even tell my husband about what happened until after my dad died because I didn't want it to affect *his* relationship with my dad. So I carried this for thirty years. We had been married for nineteen years at this point. My mom had pre-deceased my dad. After my dad died, I felt like I owed it to my husband to tell him about what had happened since it would explain some things about me and my behavior. This experience had robbed me of my innocence, the relationship a daughter should have with her father, my self-esteem, my self-worth, and I felt tremendous guilt. He said my dad probably was so ashamed of what he did that he couldn't bring himself to apologize.

Sometime after that, I attended a women's retreat and had one of those "heart-pounding" moments during a sharing time after a talk on forgiveness. I felt like the Lord wanted me to share my experience and struggle with the group. As I shared my thoughts and feelings, one lady said, "You know, if you think about it, while Jesus was hanging on the cross getting jeered at and ridiculed, and after being beaten to a pulp, He said, 'Father, forgive them, for they don't know what they are doing'" (Luke 23:34 NLT). She said, "Those people, as well as those who crucified Him, never asked for forgiveness, and yet He forgave them. You don't need your dad to ask you for forgiveness for you to forgive him."

That made sense, but I was concerned about the fact I still couldn't forget what happened and would grieve about it whenever something jogged my memory. Then I had a chance to talk to a resident counselor, and he asked me, "Would you grieve if this happened to a friend of yours?"

I said, "Of course."

He said, "It's okay to grieve over something that happened to you. That does not mean you haven't forgiven your dad." That was such a relief.

Since then, I've been able to talk about it and not get emotional. I look at it just as something that happened to me. I will never have the opportunity to test this since my dad is deceased, but I honestly think if he walked into my house, I could embrace him with a big hug and be very glad to see him. I am finally healed by forgiveness. My dad had many delightful qualities and was beloved by numerous people. This just seemed to be a flaw he had. Who knows what might have happened in *his* past to trigger this in him?

> You don't need an apology to forgive.

I know something like this can happen to a young man as well. I share all this because that evening, after I shared my story, I cannot tell you how many women came up to me with their "me too" stories. According to statistics from the National Sexual Violence Resource Center,[2] one in four girls and one in six boys are sexually abused before they are eighteen. So there is a good chance you or someone you know may have experienced something similar.

I want you to know several things:

- It is not your fault.
- You will likely grieve, re-grieve, and possibly deal with the aftereffects of trauma.
- You will most likely not forget it, but that doesn't mean you haven't forgiven your abuser.
- You don't need an apology to forgive.
- This experience is a journey, and God will help you heal over time.
- Forgiveness (when needed) is the key to freedom and happiness.
- You can get past this by obediently forgiving your offender and leaving the results to God.

Oh, the freedom and victory you will experience! Don't wait as long as I did to resolve your situation. The feelings of pain may take a while to go away, and the experience of freedom and joy may be slow in coming as it did for me, but it will happen eventually. Just trust God with it. Psalm 34:17-18 tells us: "When the righteous cry for help, the LORD hears and delivers them out of all their troubles. The LORD is near to the brokenhearted and saves the crushed in spirit."

How are you doing on the forgiveness scale right now? Would you want God to forgive you the same way you currently forgive others? Forgiveness doesn't change the past, but it does change our future!

> *Forgiveness doesn't change the past, but it does change our future!*

Diving Deeper

1. Why is forgiveness so important, and why is it so hard?

2. If we are struggling with forgiveness against another person who has wronged us, what impact does that have on our life?

3. What does forgiveness do for us?

4. Can you explain a time in your life when you forgave someone and experienced freedom?

5. Who benefits the most from forgiveness, and why?

6. How can you tell if you have truly forgiven someone?

7. What do you think was meant by the statement that we might need to be broken before God can use us?

8. What were your favorite verses in this chapter, and why?

9. How does the author's personal story tie in with the point of this chapter?

10. What is your main takeaway from this chapter? Explain.

Chapter 7

The Victorious Life Is a Gift
Let's Explore this a Little More

The victorious life can seem a bit complex and complicated to grasp. You may even want to read through this next section a couple of times to let it all sink in but stick with me here. This information is not just "gold, it's "platinum" and is well worth your time to digest it thoroughly.

Let's make sure we understand. Like our salvation, the victorious/abundant life is a gift we receive by faith and not anything we can struggle to earn on our part. All of life is a gift, both the physical and spiritual. Romans 6:23 tells us, "For the wages of sin is death, but the free gift of God is eternal life in Christ Jesus our Lord."

Eternal life does not just start when you die. It begins when Christ begins to live in you—at the time you repent of our sins and accept Him as our Lord and Savior. First John 5:11 says: "And this is the testimony, that God gave us eternal life, and this life is in His Son."

When we receive a gift, the gift itself is not gradual, but instantaneous, upon acceptance. Once we accept the Son as the *Lord* of all our being, we receive (as a gift) this eternal, victorious life. It's something God does *for* us and *in* us. (Salvation/justification is the work God does *for* us, sanctification is the work God does *in* us, and obedience is God's work *through* us.)

> *God doesn't call the qualified, He qualifies the called.*

There often is a long struggle before one is willing to surrender wholly to Christ. But this happens before the victorious life begins. Victory begins only when the struggling ceases. The moment you surrender yourself completely to Christ—when you make Him "Lord"—and look to Him in faith to dwell in your entire heart, that is the moment He comes and takes control of you.

When you decide to make this commitment, it is an act of the will, and you may not feel any different at first. Like our salvation, we must take Him at His Word and rest on that truth rather than any feelings. Can you trust His promise? Each of us must decide whether we will be totally committed and set apart for God, or content to remain living life at a lower level, not experiencing the power and intimacy possible. The difference is incomparable!

> *It's not up to us to decide how He will use us. We just need to be obedient.*

Do you understand what "crisis of belief" means? The first time I heard about that was when I read Henry Blackaby's book, *Experiencing God* many years ago. He defines it this way: "When God invites you to join him in his work, he presents a God-sized assignment that he wants to accomplish through you. It will be obvious that you can't do it on your own. If God doesn't help, you will fail. This assignment is the crisis point at which many people decide not to follow what they sense God is leading them to do. Then they wonder why they don't experience God's presence, power, and activity in their life the way that some other Christians do."[1]

What I get from this is a "faith crisis" is not necessarily anything traumatic, but part of the ongoing process of learning how to continually give ourselves over to God's plan for our lives by trusting Him for whatever it takes to carry out His will. It also involves believing He can

The Victorious Life is a Gift

and will do something through us that would otherwise seem humanly impossible.

Some biblical examples of this might be:

- God told Abraham he would father a son when he and his wife were way beyond child-bearing years.
- God told Moses he would go back to Egypt to demand Pharaoh to let the Israelites go.
- The angel told Mary she would deliver a baby who would save the world, and yet she was a virgin.
- Peter accepts Jesus's invitation to step out of the boat to join Him, walking on water.

All these and many other examples in Scripture would have been impossible, except God was involved, and it was His call in each case.

To be honest, I felt that way about writing this book. Who am I that anyone would read and believe what I say? That is my crisis of belief, my struggle. I am just a sixty-seven-year-old grandmother who loves Jesus with all her heart. I have been moved and radically changed by the message of surrender and obedience but have been fighting the call to write this book for a long time, thinking about all my inadequacies.

> *Where focus goes, energy flows, and what we focus on becomes our reality.*

I was listening to all those "wrong" voices in my head and believing them. I have recently been encouraged as I look at how God called and used simple, uneducated fishermen, tax collectors, liars, adulterers, and murders. When they were repentant, God used them, and they even ended up in the "Hall of Faith" (Hebrews 11). God can and does use anyone He chooses to accomplish His plan, and the more impossible the task, the more glory He receives as it is obviously of Him.

Someone recently reminded me that God doesn't call the qualified, He qualifies the called. When God calls, it is important to obey and leave the rest to Him and trust Him to "do His thing" whatever that might be. It's not up to us to decide how He will use us. We just need to be obedient. We'll never know how God could use us until we let Him. We might be blocking a miracle He wants to perform in or through us if we, desiring to see the result, refuse to walk in faith believing Him to act on what He has led us to do.

So, What is Obedience?

It's more than just "not sinning." It's to desire with all one's heart to walk in the center of God's will, at all times, whatever the cost. It's turning that desire into action. That is when the reward comes. Few people ever really experience that.

We need to be careful about where we maintain our focus. Where focus goes, energy flows, and what we focus on becomes our reality. When we concentrate our thoughts on our failures and the obstacles in our life, they can wrongly become exaggerated in our minds. When we fix our attention on Christ alone, and He is our focus and the desire of our heart, He is magnified and more significant in our lives. It's when we fill our minds with the thoughts of Christ that we become more like Him. When we choose to concentrate on God's truths, they will produce in us a noble character that will glorify God, which should be our goal.

It's those who embrace radical obedience who see life like few others and are drawn into the heart of God and embraced like no other. As a result, they are enticed and enabled to experience a bigger vision and are allowed to see everyday circumstances through the lens of God's perspective. When that happens, every interaction becomes a divine appointment, and every action and reaction matters.

> *It's outside our comfort zone, where we experience the pure awesomeness of God.*

Why am I bringing this up? Because the decision for holiness is a crisis—a struggle in a Christian's life. Remember how you first felt when I told you we were to be "holy?" What does a crisis of belief do? For one thing, it reminds us life is not about us. It usually takes us out of our element and refines our faith, making it real. It's outside our comfort zone, where we experience the pure awesomeness of God.

We can be sure whatever God may be calling us to do, it will be something much bigger than we are, but we also need to remember Christ has told us He will always be with us. We certainly are not alone on this journey. He is not only with us but *in* us. He wants to take us from just what we know about who God is in our head to experience who He is in our hearts. He wants to take us to the next level.

Every journey begins with the first step. We have to take that first step to get started. How we respond when God asks us to join Him in something He is doing reveals our heart. What will your response be?

With it comes an instantaneous revelation of God to us—Christ can be all in all; Christ can and does give victory over all known sin not gradually, but instantaneously. In 2 Corinthians 7:1, Paul says: "Since we have these promises, beloved, let us cleanse ourselves from every defilement of body and spirit, bringing holiness to completion in the fear of God."

Here the "fear of God" speaks of awe, reverent obedience, which is the only way of wisdom. The tense in the Greek shows this happens at once as a definite and decisive action.[2] This step of obedience is the crisis of sanctification.

After this defining step of a whole-hearted dedication of one's self to God, there comes a life-long sanctification process—a going on from strength to strength, from glory to glory. It is a process under which the believer becomes more and more conformed to Christ's life and character. That's our goal, isn't it?

> *It's when we fill our minds with the thoughts of Christ that we become more like Him.*

I have spent quite a bit of time on this because many, myself included, have made the mistake of trying to experience the process without first experiencing the crisis of sanctification. There can be little growth in grace until we have claimed by surrender and faith the "life that is Christ." Have you experienced the crisis? Have you obeyed the command as put forth by Peter in 1 Peter 3:15, "but in your hearts honor Christ the Lord as holy."

Christ is in the heart of every believer as "Savior," but is He indeed "Lord?" They are not the same thing, and just because Jesus is your Savior, does not mean He is automatically your Lord as well. It is not a question of re-conversion; it is a question of recognizing the indwelling Christ as Master in His own house—our hearts. You may have heard it said: "He must be Lord 'of all' or He is not Lord 'at all.'"

We need to remember the decision to surrender alone is not enough. That is only our part in giving up all hindrances to our blessing. If that were all we needed, then we would be making sanctification out to be merely an act of our will. We are neither saved nor sanctified by what we give up, but by what we receive.

It is the very God of peace who sanctifies us completely. After surrendering ourselves, we must look to Christ to crucify our old sinful nature and give us a new resurrected nature of life in Christ. In Jesus's death, He personified surrender. Peace is the fruit of an obedient, righteous life.

Let go—surrender. Then, let God do His part. Remember, salvation is entirely a gift of God—entirely of grace. No amount of effort or struggle on our part is allowed to help Him. Salvation is a threefold work: past, present, and future, and it's all a gift. In Romans 11:6, Paul reminds us: "But if it is by grace, it is no longer on the basis of works; otherwise grace would no longer be grace."

> *"He must be Lord 'of all' or He is not Lord 'at all.'"*

Any thought that we must contribute means it is not a gift, but a discounted purchase. When we accept Christ as Savior from the penalty of sin, we learn that even though sorrow, good resolutions, and tears often accompany repentance, His forgiveness is absolutely and entirely through faith. While it is necessary for change, repentance does not save a man. We have to leave that to Christ. Justification is entirely the work of Christ, and faith in Him secures this salvation. We can do nothing whatever to gain or merit it since it is a gift we choose to accept or reject. We also can take no credit. It is all of Christ.

When Christ comes again, that is when we will be glorified with Him. This act is the future of salvation. In this work of glorification, we also know we can do absolutely nothing. It is all of Christ.

We tend to forget all God has done for us. For a while, we're amazed and humbled when God seems to bless us. And if we're not careful to guard our hearts and minds, it's easy to begin thinking we must've done something right for Him to have been so good to us. We must be careful of that because that could lead to pride and legalism.

Let's go back to discuss our present situation more—our sanctification (which is first a crisis, and then a process). This process is what we call "the victorious life," which is probably "Experiencing the Life You Always Wanted." When we claim it by faith, then that is the crisis. When we live it day by day, that is the process. We received Jesus by simple faith; now we are to walk in Him the same way, by faith. Paul tells us in Colossians 2:6, "Therefore, as you received Christ Jesus the Lord, so walk in him." An act of faith obtains the victorious life, and we can only maintain it by a constant attitude of faith.

Before moving on, there is something I need to address. Just as Jesus was criticized, we must expect the same. The world may not see your worth, but as a Christ-follower, you are cherished by the God of the Universe! Many will not recognize the victorious life in us. They may thwart or oppose us and even deny our sincerity or beliefs. When that happens, we must maintain a spirit of humility, lacking any bitterness or spiritual pride. Otherwise, our victory is broken. We are sure to be misunderstood and not just by unbelievers.

Believe it or not, some of our greatest opponents and critics will be within the church. Every church has its back-biters and hypocrites who like to stir up trouble. These are instruments of Satan. The servant is not greater than his Master. If Christ received opposition from "religious" as well as "non-religious" people, so shall we.

Peace is the fruit of an obedient, righteous life.

This provides an opportunity to show, not so much by our words, but demonstrating with humility, the Christ-life to prove there *is* victory through the Lord Jesus Christ. Take courage that others will see our victory through Christ and will rejoice because they will see the mighty power of God at work. Humility has little to do with how we feel but has a lot to do with where our focus is and how we treat others.

The Victorious Life is a Gift

There is no harder lesson to learn than that of humility. It is not taught in the schools of men, only in the school of Christ. It is the rarest of all the gifts. Very rarely do we find a man or woman who is following closely the footsteps of the Master in meekness and in humility. I believe that it is the hardest lesson which Jesus Christ had to teach His disciples while He was here upon earth. It almost looked at first as though He had failed to teach it to the twelve men who had been with Him almost constantly for three years.

I believe if we can be humble enough, we will be sure to get a great blessing. After all, I think that more depends upon us than upon the Lord because He is always ready to give a blessing and give it freely, but we are not always in a position to receive it. He always blesses the humble, and if we can get down in the dust before Him, no one will go away dissatisfied.[3]

Jesus Christ can free and deliver us from the power of self. He only asks that we humble ourselves before Him. I believe it is one of the most prominent, foundational virtues of Christianity. It is the first character quality commanded in the beatitudes (Matthew 5:3-12) and describes the noble grace of Christ.

"Someone asked Augustine, what was the first of the religious graces, and he said, 'Humility.' They asked him what the second was, and he replied, 'Humility.' They asked him the third, and he said, 'Humility.' It looks like if we are humble, we have all the graces."[4] We must be careful, though. The minute we think we are humble, we have lost it.

Humility has little to do with how we feel but has a lot to do with where our focus is and how we treat others.

A person can counterfeit love, faith, and even hope and all the other graces, but it is tough to counterfeit humility. If we want to appeal to the God of Heaven, we must humble ourselves, and if we do humble ourselves before the Lord, we will not be disappointed. He reminds us in Mark 10:43–44, "...whoever would be great among you must be your servant, and whoever would be first among you must be slave of all."

> *The minute we think we are humble, we have lost it.*

Paul calls us to follow Christ's example of the suffering servant if we remember in Philippians 2:1-11, where we read Jesus came not to be served but to serve. He is our ultimate example of humility.

DIVING DEEPER

1. When do we experience eternal life, and what is that all about?

2. What is a "Crisis of belief," and what does it do? Can you explain a time when you went through such a crisis?

3. Define Christian obedience, as explained in this chapter. Is there an area of your life where you struggle with that? Please share such a struggle or an area in which you have experienced success.

4. Why is it important for us to maintain our focus on the Lord and positive influences?

5. Have you seen a shift at all in your understanding of Jesus being Lord as well as Savior in your life? Can you explain the difference?

6. How are we sanctified in Christ? Can you explain the process and what part we play in that? Where and how does faith come in?

7. How does humility fit in with the Christian life, and why is it so important?

8. What were the most meaningful verses to you in this chapter, and why?

9. What were the main points or takeaways for you in this chapter?

10. What is one key truth from this chapter you sense the Spirit is urging you to embrace and act on?

Chapter 8

Still Feel Like You're Struggling with Known Sin?

If you're still feeling defeated, you are a victim of Satan, the accuser, which causes you to feel like you are a loser or not enough—attacking your vulnerable areas. You certainly are not alone in that. We've all been there. May I gently remind you that struggling, striving, and agonizing over sin is a lack of trust in Christ's ability to save you from the power of any sin? He can and wants to "kill" it for you. He has already conquered the power of sin and Satan when He rose from the dead. He *is* the conqueror.

Lamentations 3:22–23 says: "The steadfast love of the LORD never ceases; his mercies never come to an end; they are new every morning; great is your faithfulness."

I have a friend who is always saying, "Thank the Lord; it's a 'Do-over' day." When you realize you have messed up, think about the Etch-a-Sketch you probably had as a child. When you messed up, all you had to do was turn it upside down and shake it, erasing what you had created. Then you could start over. A clean slate is possible!

Jesus is closer to you than your nearest and dearest earthly friend.

Romans 6:14 reminds us, "For sin will have no dominion over you, since you are not under law but under grace." Romans 8:37 reminds us: "... in all these things we are more than conquerors through him who loved us."

This refers not only to our current bothersome sin but also our desire to sin can also be taken away. Please remember the famous verse, Philippians 4:13: "I can do all things through him who strengthens me." Let's also remember and Hebrews 13:5: "...I will never leave you nor forsake you."

> *We are best helped when we recognize we are helpless.*

Jesus is closer to you than your nearest and dearest earthly friend. By now, you have realized you cannot eradicate sin from your life by your efforts, but Christ will keep safe every life who trusts Him from the power of sin.

If your defense is about your weakness, remember 2 Corinthians 12:9 where Paul quoted God's response when he asked that He remove the "thorn in his flesh," "...'My grace is sufficient for you, for my power is made perfect in weakness.' Therefore I will boast all the more gladly of my weaknesses, so that the power of Christ may rest upon me."

We can be kept safe only by the power of God through faith. Whether we have faith in something or not will not alter the truth about it. God's grace is always sufficient—no matter what our needs. God, Himself, has declared it so.

May I encourage you if you feel like you are at the end of yourself and wonder how you can surrender to God at every moment of every day during trials and temptations, then you are on the right track. We are best helped when we recognize we are helpless.

Just confess your heart's desire is to learn what it looks like to be totally surrendered, but feel helpless to accomplish it. Then ask the Lord to enable you to live like Christ. Remember, what is impossible with us is possible with God; with God, all things are possible!

Obedience is a response that comes from your heart. If you find yourself struggling to obey God, then that is a clear warning your heart has shifted away from Him. If you truly love Jesus, you will obey Him. Love is the discipline. He looks past your godly, moral lifestyle, and even your ministry involvement and focuses His attention on your heart.

> *Obedience is a response that comes from your heart.*

If you find yourself continually falling into sinful habits and not grieving over your sin, this would indicate you are not abiding in Christ. He certainly is not Lord. Just return to Him in repentance, and He will restore the fellowship you once experienced, and you will once again experience victory in your life. He will never turn down that type of prayer!

If you struggle to believe, that is not the time to pull away from Christ or be ashamed of your struggle. The only way we can strengthen our faith is to reach out to Jesus, not retreat! Jesus wants to help you with your belief. He will meet your need, but He also will give you the faith to trust Him to provide for you. Go to Him and allow Him to convince you of His ability to meet every need you will ever face.

Just like we cannot take a day off morally and stay moral, we cannot take a day off spiritually and remain spiritual. God wants us to be entirely His, and that takes a lot of time and effort living intentionally. Often we want to take shortcuts. We want mountaintop experiences without going through the valleys. It doesn't work that way. We need to learn to abide.

> *Just like we cannot take a day off morally and stay moral, we cannot take a day off spiritually and remain spiritual.*

God allows failure so we can understand and come to terms with knowing we alone have *no* power. It's through these difficult times we can come to terms with our sinfulness. It's God's way of reminding us how unregenerate we are and helpless without Him.

If you are struggling with surrender, I have a story for you. Maybe you've heard of the story about Jenny's pearls? I'm not sure where this story originated but is a classic example of the blessing of surrender.

The story goes something like this:

> Jenny was five years old, and one day when shopping with her mom, she eyed a set of plastic pearls at the store checkout counter. She just had to have them. Her mother told her she could earn the two dollars they cost. When she finally could purchase them, she wore them everywhere and was so proud of her beautiful pearls.
>
> Her daddy would come in and tuck her in at night, and after reading her a bedtime story, he would ask her, "Do you love me?"
>
> Jenny would always reply, "Yes, Daddy, you know I love you."
>
> "Then give me your pearls," he would say.
>
> "Oh no, Daddy, please, not my pearls, but you can have…" and she would offer one of her favorite toys.
>
> "That's okay," her dad would say. "I love you. Good night." And he would give her a good night kiss.
>
> This exchange went on for several nights. Finally, one night, when her daddy came in, she was sitting cross-

legged in her bed, and her little chin was quivering, and a tear was rolling down her cheek.

Her dad said, "What is it, Jenny? What's the matter?"

She didn't say a thing, but lifted her little head to her daddy and handed the string of tiny plastic pearls, saying, "Here Daddy, these are for you." As he held back his tears, he took the beads, reached into his pocket, brought out a blue velvet box with a strand of genuine pearls, and gave them to her. He had them all along and was just waiting for his little girl to give up the cheap stuff so he could bless her with the genuine treasure.

So it is with our loving heavenly Father. He is patiently waiting for us to give up the unimportant things in our lives so He can give us beautiful treasures. Isn't God good? He only wants the best for us. Are you holding onto anything which God wants you to let go? Power in this life comes from letting go and letting God do His thing.

Have you ever experienced washing the car or watering your garden, and suddenly, the water flow stops? You look over and see the faucet is still turned on, so the water source is still active, but then you look again and see a kink in the hose, causing the flow to stop. What is the kink in your hose that is shutting off the power of God in your life?

He will never take away something without ultimately giving you something much better in its place.

Are you holding onto hurtful, toxic, or unnecessary relationships, habits, and activities to which you have become so attached it seems impossible to let go? Do you realize these are the things that hold you back from experiencing the best from God? Sometimes it is hard to know what God might have in store for you, but do believe this one thing—He will never take away something without ultimately giving you something much better in its place.

Still Feel like You're Struggling with Known Sin?

Diving Deeper

1. Looking over this and previous chapters, how is it Satan tries to rob us of our joy and make us feel defeated?

2. What are some lessons we can learn from our failures?

3. Debby stated, "God's grace is sufficient." Can you expand on that statement to explain the meaning of grace, how we get it, and what it means in the Christian life?

4. How have you seen Jesus come in and rescue you, a friend, or family member from a prevailing or recurring sin? Can you explain what happened?

5. What is the main point of this chapter? What lesson(s) do you see?

LIVING THE LIFE YOU ALWAYS WANTED

6. What area of your life to you see you need to be more willing to surrender? What changes are necessary, and what will the cost be to follow through on that?

7. Based on what we have learned so far, what do you see as bene7. s of surrender?

8. What are some steps we can take when feeling defeated in our sin?

9. Why do you think we find surrender so difficult?

10. There are a lot of great verses in this short chapter. Which ones are the most meaningful and speak most to your heart?

11. Are you ready at this point to write a blank check to God to let Him do whatever He wants in your life? Are you "All In?"

Chapter 9

How Does Suffering Fit in With a Victorious Life?

No one likes storms that come to us in life; however, we must remember God is sovereign, His plan is perfect, and He is in control of all things. Many times God allows failure, pain, and suffering in some form so we can experience Him through the storm.

A common question I often get is: "Why does God allow so much suffering in the world?" That's a loaded question, and whole books have been written on that topic, but suffice it to say, God can and does allow all kinds of suffering and redeems it for good in our lives. I'm sure you are familiar with Romans 8:28, where Paul tells us: "And we know that for those who love God all things work together for good, for those who are called according to his purpose."

This verse does not in any way imply everything that happens to us is good, but rather God has a way of making good come even from things that may seem bad to us at the time. He doesn't waste the pain, and we can learn so much from it if we allow ourselves to be teachable.

> *Many times God allows failure, pain, and suffering in some form so we can experience Him through the storm.*

As Christ-followers, we have to remember we can trust Him to have our best interests in mind in all things. He has a purpose, and His plans to accomplish His purposes are perfect. Sometimes He not only allows but causes adversity to happen so we can see Him at work to redeem a situation which increases our faith and gives Him glory. Seeking to understand this helps us to change our perspective to align with His.

> *If we never had troubles or pain of any kind, we would not come to appreciate God's presence through hardship.*

If we never had troubles or pain of any kind, we would not come to appreciate God's presence through hardship. If we never had any challenges in life, we would become self-reliant, self-dependent, and think we had everything under control. It's the difficult times that cause us to turn to the Lord for help, comfort, strength, wisdom, and guidance. Sometimes remembering our need to trust and lean into Christ is what we need more than anything. Sometimes God lets us experience a stressful situation rather than rescuing us from it because He knows we will come out stronger on the other side.

A lot of the things we experience in life as a believer are counter-cultural, meaning they defy logic. We often try to avoid trials, suffering, and persecution, but those are the things that produce abundant joy in us. With God's help, we are more than conquerors in all things—not in spite of them but in the midst of them. Our joy in the Lord is not regardless of our trials but because of them!

> *Sometimes remembering our need to trust and lean into Christ is what we need more than anything.*

God can build some things in our lives *only* through suffering. Some places in our soul can only be reached by suffering, and some lessons we can only learn during trials. We should not resent the suffering God allows in our life and invest all we have to avoid hardship—trying to manipulate situations in

How Does Suffering Fit in with a Victorious Life?

Sometimes God lets us experience a stressful situation rather than rescuing us from it because He knows we will come out stronger on the other side.

our own strength. God didn't spare His own Son, so why should we expect Him to spare us? We need to be willing to learn obedience, even when it hurts.

It's also what draws us to Him for help and comfort in our time of need. We can count on God to carry us through even the most difficult times, and if we let Him, He can and will turn bad to good. We may not always see how He uses it. He might use *how* we respond to a particular problem to influence others positively, which could encourage them in their faith or even lead them to salvation.

He can and will use adversity to teach and grow us in ways we would never have if the difficulty had never come. God doesn't always tell us why He allows (physical, spiritual, emotional) wounds. We may feel for a time God is absent and question why certain things occur. He may let something happen we don't understand, which may have protected us from something far worse. We need to learn to trust Him in all things.

This may seem like a simplistic example, but when you are frustrated that a person on their cell phone isn't paying attention at the stoplight, causing you to miss the green light, that delay just might have prevented you from being in an accident.

I don't need to tell you we live in a "fallen" world where sin is rampant. Often we are living an obedient life and are caused what seems to be undue suffering at the hands of someone else's sin and disobedience. It feels so wrong, and the pain can seem unbearable. When things like that happen, you can be sure God grieves with you.

"What matters in life is not so much what happens to us, but what happens in us."

There is no pain so deeply embedded in your heart, God's grace cannot reach down and at least provide comfort, if not eradicate it over time.

God grants everyone "free choice," and sometimes many abuse that privilege affecting innocent people. God will not force Himself on anyone, and we share space on this planet with those individuals, the result of which often leads to pain.

I remember a time when my dad was passed over for a promotion. He and my mom were very upset, as they honestly believed my dad deserved it more than the gentleman who received it in his place. Not long after that, the Army went through a RIF (Reduction in Forces), and many top-ranking officers were separated from the military against their wishes. This gentleman who received the promotion in my dad's place was discharged with no retirement. My dad just had to wait another year to get his promotion. If he had been promoted when he thought he deserved it, he would have been discharged too early to receive his retirement. What seemed unfair ended up being God's protection.

God can build some things in our lives only through suffering.

Remember, in the book of Acts in the New Testament, when Stephen, a leader in the early Christian church, was unjustly accused and martyred for his faith? The disciples and other believers had been hanging out in Jerusalem and not going to the ends of the earth, spreading the gospel as Christ had commanded them in Matthew 28 just before He ascended. When Stephen got stoned, persecution became rampant, and the Christians scattered to other regions and countries to escape maltreatment. They spread the gospel wherever they went, which is how others learned about Christ. So while

We need to be willing to learn obedience, even when it hurts.

How Does Suffering Fit in with a Victorious Life?

"No pit is so deep that He is not deeper still."

Stephen's stoning was a horrible thing to witness, look at the good that came from it. As the believers fled persecution, it caused the gospel to get spread throughout the land. He got to go to heaven early to be with Jesus and suffered no more persecution.

If you think long and hard enough, you can think of situations where you felt a circumstance seemed impossible or unfair, yet God worked it out for good. But, as I mentioned earlier, even though we might not see how God works in this lifetime, we can trust He always has our best interests at heart and doesn't waste any experiences.

No doubt and no exception, we all experience suffering in this life, but we need to look at trials and tribulations like converting stumbling blocks into stepping stones. They are opportunities for growth as we surrender those situations to Jesus and let Him in His sovereignty do whatever is necessary to use those circumstances to grow us in our faith and character, as we trust Him in His faithfulness to see us through. How is God building your character?

How Do We Respond to Suffering?

We cannot control our circumstances, but we can control how we respond to them. We can control whether an experience makes us bitter or better. To quote Rick Warren, "What matters in life is not so much what happens *to* us, but what happens *in* us."[1] If we become bitter over our hardships, we close part of our lives from God, and we will never be complete.

"Our capacity for pain is a measure of our potential for growth."

It allows us to evaluate if we are relying too much on self-trust or leaning on Jesus to provide us with the strength to muscle through difficult times. Roots grow deep when the wind is strong. What I desire for all of us are "Deep Roots" that allow us to process the suffering in our lives to make us become like Jesus.

> *Some lessons can only be learned through trials.*

Sometimes—most times, it's hard to see pain as a gift, but it actually can be when it causes us to turn to Christ. It shifts our focus from ourselves to Him. To quote Betsy Ten Boom, Corrie's sister, while in the concentration camp: "No pit is so deep that He is not deeper still."[2]

There is no area in our life so painful God's grace cannot bring healing. If there never was any pain, trial, or temptations, and all our life-experience was a total success as *we* define it, we would feel self-sufficient and would never appreciate our need for Jesus. I once heard Joel Houston of Hillsong Church say, "Our capacity for pain is a measure of our potential for growth."

Christ may lead you into what may seem like impossible situations, but you need to embrace them rather than avoid them. Stay in the fray because that is where you will experience God.

Some lessons can only be learned through trials. We must learn to exercise obedience, even when it hurts. God's will for you may involve some hardship as it did for Jesus, but He loves you, and with His help, He will not allow you to experience more than you can handle.

One thing we can count on is while Christ could calm the storm (and sometimes He does), often He wants us to see Him as our peace in the storm. He has the power over anything of which we might be afraid. If we focus on our problems, they may appear enormous. But as we focus on God, we can see our situation in the proper perspective and be assured all things are possible with God. Joy is not the absence of suffering, but the presence of God. He won't necessarily take away our problems but will carry us through the difficulty, no matter what.

There is a famous poem you are probably familiar with, but it seems appropriate to share it here as it fits in well with our discussion about God's presence during hardship.

Joy is not the absence of suffering, but the presence of God.

Footprints in the Sand[3]
By Mary Stevenson (1936)

One night I dreamed a dream.

As I was walking along the beach with my Lord,

Across the dark sky flashed scenes from my life.

For each scene, I noticed two sets of footprints in the sand,

One belonging to me and one to my Lord.

After the last scene of my life flashed before me,

I looked back at the footprints in the sand.

I noticed that at many times along the path of my life,

especially at the very lowest and saddest times,

there was only one set of footprints.

This really troubled me, so I asked the Lord about it.

"Lord, you said once I decided to follow you,

You'd walk with me all the way.

But I noticed that during the saddest and most troublesome times of my life,

there was only one set of footprints.

I don't understand why, when I needed You the most, You would leave me."

He whispered, "My precious child, I love you and will never leave you.

Never, ever, during your trials and testings.

When you saw only one set of footprints,

It was then that I carried you."

He tells us to lean on Him. "Come to me, all who labor and are heavy laden, and I will give you rest. Take my yoke upon you, and learn from me, for I am gentle and lowly in heart, and you will find rest for your souls. For my yoke is easy, and my burden is light" (Matthew 11:28–30).

He wants us to rest in Him, to trust in Him, knowing His ways are better than our ways, and His thoughts greater than our thoughts (Isaiah 55:9). He knows so much better what we need than we do. He wants to bless us, but sometimes we have to go through a process of surrender and obedience before experiencing those blessings.

How Does Suffering Fit in with a Victorious Life?

You may be familiar with a contemporary song by Hillary Scott called, "Thy Will Be Done."[4] You can check it out on YouTube. I think you will find the lyrics fit in well with what I've been discussing here. I will put the link in the resources section in the back of this book.

I have a friend who discipled me in college and was instrumental in getting me on fire for the Lord and studying the Bible through which I started to understand God's heart. This experience was forty-eight years ago. She just found out she has stage 4 lung cancer, and it has metastasized to her brain and abdomen. She started treatment right away after being pretty much asymptomatic. Her only clue something might be wrong was a balance issue. She has never smoked and leads a healthy lifestyle, so obviously, this was an incredible shocker.

I'm telling you this because I want to share with you how a person living the victorious life can handle such devastating news and emerge from it with the joy of the Lord as her strength. It was incredibly inspiring to me, and I hope it will also be for you as you witness through her testimony here what it's like to be "all in" for Christ.

Here is a quote from her Facebook page after she shared her news:

I am at such peace. This has actually been one of the best weeks of my life. I have focused on what is really important, sat around with my family and laughed and laughed (and cried, too). All I want to do is visit with friends. God has been sooooo good to me all my life. He is holding me in the palm of His hand at every turn." She put up a graphic with this which read, "It Is Well with My Soul."

She got that phrase from a famous hymn. If you're a Christian, you're probably familiar with the old hymn, "It is Well with My Soul." You may know the story too, but it bears repeating, especially if you are not familiar with it. It exemplifies the life of someone who knows how to put their trust in God and can rest in His sovereignty. It also is an example of how someone can have peace in the midst of probably one of the worst nightmares a parent could ever experience.

Horatio Spafford was a prominent, successful lawyer in 1871 when the historical Chicago fire destroyed most of his holdings and investments. When the dust settled, he decided he needed to take some time off with his family and go to Europe for a couple of months just to recoup mentally and emotionally from what happened and regain perspective. He booked passage on a boat for himself, his wife, and their four daughters. About the time to leave, he became aware of a zoning problem of some of his properties and decided he needed to stay behind to resolve. So he sent the family ahead and said he would catch the next ship.

The ship carrying his family sank as it was hit by another ship, the *Loch Earn*, and all four daughters drowned. Maybe you've heard of that famous telegram his wife sent. It simply stated, "Saved alone." A few weeks later, he boarded a ship to join his wife, and when his ship was crossing the area where the previous ship went down, the captain told Horatio, "This is the place where you lost your daughters."

As he looked over the ocean, with the spirit of God speaking into the deepest part of his soul, he penned the words of that now famous, emotionally stirring hymn. There are six verses to this song that glorify God, and in its entirety, it encapsulates the gospel story. As words of encouragement, it is often sung at Christian funerals. For brevity here, I will just quote the first three verses as they explain the point about peace during life's storms. I believe they demonstrate his knowledge of the gospel and his relationship with Christ, which gave him the strength to write these words with such internal conviction and peace. Totally amazing in my mind! What grace he experienced from God as He met him in his sorrow.

It is Well with My Soul

By Horatio Spafford

Verse 1:

When peace like a river, attendeth my way.

When sorrows like sea billows roll,

Whatever my lot, Thou has taught me to say,

It is well, it is well with my soul.

(Refrain:)

It is well (it is well) with my soul (with my soul)

It is well, it is well, with my soul

Verse 2:

Though Satan should buffet, though trials should come,

Let this blest assurance control,

That Christ hath regarded my helpless estate,

And hath shed His own blood for my soul.

(Refrain)

Verse 3:

My sin, oh the bliss of this glorious thought!
My sin, not in part, but the whole,
Is nailed to His cross, and I bear it no more,
Praise the Lord, praise the Lord, O my soul!
(Refrain)

This is not a theory. This is real stuff we're dealing with here. I'm sure all of us have had a good reason for fear, anxiety, or depression based on our life's experience. If we haven't, we will. It's just a matter of time when we will be faced with some tragedy or challenge in which we will have to choose how to react or respond. I'm sure we all have experienced the grief of financial loss or the loss of a loved one. What do we do with that? We can drown in despair, or we can choose peace. We will discuss that at length in the next chapter.

Here's a later post from my friend just a couple of weeks out from her diagnosis:

TODAY I STARTED SCRATCHING THINGS OFF MY BUCKET LIST

It's not because I have accomplished them. But because they really don't matter anymore. My husband and I were supposed to fly to Anchorage, Alaska, today where we would take a five-day land tour up to Denali National Park and then join life-long friends for a cruise down the Inside Passage to Vancouver.

After receiving news of a Stage 4 cancer diagnosis, I have a new bucket list. It now includes things like: watch my grandsons play baseball. See my granddaughter in a dance recital. Watch my youngest grandson take his first steps. A cruise down the Danube or a return trip to Yellowstone would be nice, but I'll take my new list now. It includes:

- Get my affairs in order
- Adjust to the "new normal" lifestyle of living with cancer
- Down-size, simplify, de-clutter my house, life, and thoughts
- Take a picture with my dear family
- Celebrate the fact that fifty years ago my name was written in the Lamb's Book of Life
- Follow the best treatment protocol for my recovery
- Go on a spa getaway with my two lovely daughters and laugh, talk, and snuggle together
- Have quality time with each of my five grandchildren and let them know how special they are to me
- Write down or record as many of the blessings God has given me over my life
- Have special times with my husband as we enjoy get-togethers with life-long friends
- Celebrate my sixty-ninth birthday in two months
- Visit my brother and sister and all my family and friends
- Let all the wonderful friends I have, know how much I treasure their friendship
- Fight the good fight
- Summer 2020 Go with the whole family to Hilton Head
- Run with endurance the race set before me for however long the Lord wants me here
- Finish the race and fall into the arms of Jesus

- Be part of the welcoming committee in heaven and eagerly wait for those I love and care about. People like you.

Wow, no one can say all that unless they are surrendered and empowered by the love of Christ! I know the news of her diagnosis has been devastating to her family and friends who love her so much, and I know she would like to live to old age with her family and watch her grandkids grow up, get married, and so on. However, her countenance exudes the joy of the Lord. She is one with Christ and surrendered to whatever His plan is for her.

Who knows? Maybe God will choose to heal her, either miraculously or through medical treatment, but she is surrendered to whatever God's plan is for her. This is what we call "grace," which God has given her in her time of need—the ability to persevere under a tremendous trial.

Onlookers find it remarkable how she can be so radiant in the light of her news; however, her trust and faith are in her Lord. He is using her as a witness to many who see her posts and family photos on Facebook and to all the hospital personnel tending to her. She would tell you even if one person gave their life to Christ as a result of her situation and witness, it was worth it.

When we allow God to take charge of us in Christ, He can make us a man or woman of absolute, total surrender, and He can maintain it. He can enable us to rise every morning with the assurance He, in the person of the Holy Spirit, is in charge, working out our life for us.

I try to start my day before I get out of bed with a thanksgiving prayer for a good night's sleep and the new day. Then I ask the Holy Spirit to fill me with Himself and remind me of His presence throughout the day, to direct my path to make the most of it to fulfill His will.

When you trust Him to do His work in you, it's impressive all the things you can accomplish, you thought were impossible, like loving the unlovely. Remember, God *is* love, and God is *in* you helping you to love perfectly. What an amazing ride—and the "joy," oh, the joy of the Lord is such a strength and gives amazing power to overcome so much.

While the Holy Spirit is in the heart of every believer, He often is forgotten, grieved, quenched, and dishonored to the point He cannot do His work. God loves to fill His children with His Spirit and longs to give each of us His power for our daily life. He wants us to confess our sins before Him daily and to call on Him for mercy.

Since we began in the Spirit at our conversion, why is it we tend to take over trying to run out the rest of our life in the flesh—in our own strength? That is why we so often experience failure. The Spirit of God was given to us with the expectation we would always live our lives in the power of the Holy Spirit. He delights in helping us and will enable us to perfect in the Spirit what was begun in the Spirit. We are encouraged by the psalmist in Psalm 55:22, to "Cast your burden upon the LORD, and he will sustain you; he will never permit the righteous to be shaken (NASB). Christ is not just our sin-bearer, but also our burden-bearer. "Surely he has borne our griefs and carried our sorrows" (Isaiah 53:4).

We live in a world full of such sin and sorrow in which Satan is alive and well and on the move. Remember, for you, Christ is on the throne and is stronger; in fact, He has already claimed victory. We just need to go about our work clothed with the humility of Christ, with a broken and contrite heart, and more dependent on Him than ever. Our most significant hindrance to trust is our self-effort. Praise God; we can accomplish so much through Him if we trust Him, wait on Him, and allow Him to do His work through us. Our God delights to help us.

I would like to end this section by sharing my take on one of Jesus's parables found in Matthew 13:44. Here Jesus talks about a man who found a hidden treasure in a field. He knew it to be of great value, so he hid the treasure again, went home, and sold all he had to purchase the field. He knew the hidden treasure was worth far more than the cost of the field.

Jesus is speaking here of salvation (giving all we have and are in exchange for His saving grace). However, it could just as well apply to the victorious life. Once we learn the power (the treasure) of a surrendered life, we realize the benefits far outweigh the sacrifice.

Diving Deeper

1. Why does God allow suffering?

2. What would happen to us if we never experienced suffering?

3. Has something ever happened to you or someone you know that you thought was a tragedy, but later learned or decided was a blessing in disguise at the time? Explain.

4. How do you respond to difficult times? Do you get angry and blame God, or do you look to God asking for answers for lessons to learn? Explain some personal experiences and maybe different outcomes based on your response(s).

5. Can you explain a time when God used a difficult situation to teach you some valuable lessons? Did you find yourself becoming bitter during that time, or was it a time you came to trust Him more as a result of what you went through? Maybe a combination of both as you went through the process? Please explain.

6. Have you experienced hardship for standing up to your beliefs? How has God blessed your obedience to that?

7. Debby has stressed the importance of paying attention to what we focus on. What are the lessons learned from that?

8. Paul tells us in Romans 6:3-5 we are to rejoice in our sufferings. Explain what he means by that, and how have you personally experienced that in your life?

9. What did you think about Debby's friend who is going through cancer right now? How are you inspired and encouraged by her testimony? How do you think you would respond to that diagnosis? After what you have read so far, do you think you are now better equipped to have a similar response? In what way?

10. What is your takeaway from the Horatio Spafford story, and how can you use that in your life?

Chapter 10

What Are You Afraid Of?

At the time of this writing, our world is experiencing a global crisis—a worldwide pandemic of a new coronavirus (COVID-19). There is no cure, and any hope for a vaccine is in the distant future. So far, there have been many millions of cases globally, including over five million in the United States and well over 180,000 deaths, also in the US. Those numbers continue to climb. Travel has been restricted, and people have been ordered to stay home unless they have to go out for medical reasons, groceries, or to work.

Most people, if they can, work from home. If we go anywhere, we are expected to wear a face mask and keep a physical distance of at least six feet. Many commodities we usually take for granted have become scarce or prices have skyrocketed. Schools and businesses have shut down, and travel has been majorly restricted. Unemployment has hit an all-time high, and the stock market has tanked. We are told this is far from over, and we could easily have a reoccurrence as restrictions are lifted. This is unnerving since people need to go back to work. The economy is in a recession.

If we ever lived in an uncertain time with an unclear future and reason to fear, it is now. We need to watch enough news to be informed and know how we need to respond based on public health experts' advice, but that is enough to cause even the most stable individual to have significant concerns. Fear is a natural response for humans and has its place to help keep us safe. However, living in fear is counter-productive and is not an option if we will get through this or any other difficult circumstance. We cannot allow ourselves to get stuck there and dwell on negative issues.

Individuals experience fear and even depression for many reasons, and our world seems to be growing more and more fearful every day. The news media is adept at covering the goriest of details that bring violent crimes into our homes, feeding the trough of human despair. Suicides have become commonplace—even on the rise, especially among the youth, while disease, accidents, death, social unrest, and corruption personify our broken, fallen world. This has hit very close for me as I just lost a friend to suicide due to anxiety and depression last week.

What Is Fear?

Merriam-Webster's dictionary says fear is "an unpleasant, often strong emotion caused by anticipation or awareness of danger; it's an anxious concern or reason for alarm, or to be afraid or apprehensive."[1] What are *you* afraid of? What gives *you* anxiety and sleepless nights? Is it your future, your health, your marriage, your children, aging parents, your employment? The list goes on. It's different for everyone. If you are experiencing any form of anxiety, fear, depression, uncertainty, or dread, please realize you are not alone. This is a normal phenomenon that everyone experiences at some point in their life.

There is no question we are living in very uncertain times of great need, and it is so easy to feel overwhelmed.

Believe it or not, there is a way to experience peace in the midst of all this, and that is what I will be unpacking in this chapter. We have many choices in life. Every day we're making more choices than we realize. Peace is another choice we can make over fear, depression, and anxiety.

> *He is for us and wants to be our fortress to provide whatever we need to be comforted.*

It takes recognizing where our mind is going and living with the intention to make a U-turn and choosing peace. That takes focusing on the God who created you and trusting He is the one in control of all things, even though it may not seem so at times. He lets us experience all kinds of trials and turmoil, and He has His reasons for doing so. As I mentioned previously, if we never had any difficulty, we would feel pretty self-sufficient with no need to turn to Him for guidance and direction. We would not realize He has so much more for us!

If you look at the Psalms, you will see David and other writers crying out to God in fear, agony, and despair, even asking Him sometimes if He had deserted them because He seemed so far away. When going through something like this, it is easy to get a warped view of God if we are not reading Scripture (the Word of God), and claiming His promises. Even the Psalms, which can be heavy with honest hopelessness, can be the best antidepressant, full of encouragement at the same time as the psalmists pour out their hearts to God and learn to put their trust in Him. There is no question we are living in very uncertain times of great need, and it is so easy to feel overwhelmed.

You know what, though, there have always been times like this which we discover as we study the Scriptures, especially the Psalms. I am reminded of where we need to go and who to focus on in times like these. David tells us in Psalm 46:1, "God is our refuge and strength, a very present help in trouble." This whole psalm is a great one to bring comfort when fearful. It starts with this comforting promise and ends with a promise as well as a reminder for us to rest in Him in verse 10, "Be still, and know that I am God."

He is *for* us and wants to be our fortress to provide whatever we need to be comforted. He is our strength—our internal strength to endure. When we are open to Him, He gives us grace in the moment, just when we need it. We don't know what tomorrow holds. All we need to do is to trust Him for today. He tells us in this psalm and many other places in Scripture that He, the Lord our God, is there for us in our time of trouble, our time of need.

During these times of despair, we need to change our perspective to remember the sovereignty of God, and how good, holy, and righteous His is—full of grace, mercy, forgiveness, and truth. We need to trust Him completely, remembering He is faithful, unchanging, and in control, even though it may not seem so. We need to take our eyes off our troubles and remember all the ways God has blessed us and be grateful for the blessings and rainbows we have experienced during our past storms. If we have a big God, His presence can give us an inner sense of peace and joy, even during difficult times.

> *If we have a big God, His presence can give us an inner sense of peace and joy, even during difficult times.*

WHAT IS DEPRESSION?

Let's talk about depression for a minute since it is so rampant and not well understood regarding its causes and remedies. Depression, according to Webster's dictionary, is "a mood disorder marked especially by sadness, inactivity, difficulty in thinking and concentration, a significant increase or decrease in appetite and time spent sleeping, feelings of dejection and hopelessness, and sometimes suicidal tendencies."[2] Depression is not necessarily caused by sin, but it can be.

What are some causes for depression? There are two false beliefs that I know of for sure. Some, based on their life-experience and circumstances may believe, "I'm not wanted or needed by anyone. My life has no purpose or meaning. I am a victim of an uncaring world that brings me pain." The other myth causing despair might be that "significance and meaning comes from life and when goals achieved don't bring the happiness expected, there can be a feeling of what's the point of continuing—it's like chasing after the wind."

While we're talking all this doom and gloom, let's go over some depression symptoms just to make sure we don't leave anyone out. According to a podcast I heard by pastor, Chip Ingram, someone who is depressed may very well have feelings of hopelessness and apathy and find it difficult to concentrate. At the root of depression is a loss of perspective. There are often physical side effects, including sleeplessness, loss of appetite, or an uncontrollable urge to eat everything in sight. Sometimes there is a loss of sex drive, low self-esteem, desire to withdraw from relationships, fantasy thinking about escaping, and isolating. Occasionally, these feelings can include over sensitivity to what others do, inappropriate anger, guilt, and not liking oneself, feeling a need for help, but then feeling even more helpless as others may *try* to help. Have I covered everyone yet? Have you seen yourself? Are you depressed yet?

Unresolved sin and guilt before God will bring about depression. It can just be the revelation of a need in one's life, the result of which has distorted reality and self-worth. It also can serve as a red flag to indicate help is needed to explore what is amiss. If we recognize and admit our need for help, we can grow from the process. It's essential to be proactive in getting the support we need to resolve these self-defeating emotions; otherwise, they will just fester and grow.

There are three causes of depression: physical, psychological (emotional), and spiritual. If you are clinically depressed, some neurological things are going on in your brain, and clarity is often absent, keeping you from thinking clearly. You could be on antidepressants.

The number one drug sold in America is antidepressants. Sometimes medication *is* necessary to help you get your brain back on track so you can start working on your issues. Multiple physical problems can contribute to depression as well, and even the medications for those medical issues can be a cause for depression. In these cases, praying isn't the only answer. However, we need to be careful not to use medication as an excuse, substitute, or denial for the need to work on our spiritual life to get things right with God.

Because of something I witnessed recently, I feel the need to include something rather heavy here about depression because it is very real. I will discuss "anxiety" in the next section, but I'd like to discuss "angst" right now. Angst is deep anxiety and dread that can migrate into despair and on into depression. Someone who has "angst" about something has an unfocused sense of apprehension of the state of the world and their own future.

Life appears meaninglessness and pointless. Hopelessness sets in with despair and despondency with thoughts that things will never get better. When a person loses hope like that, that is when horrendous things happen. This is not always the case, but many have stated that their hopelessness came from lack of religion and lack of meaning that there is a God and that there something more than themselves.

If someone seems to have become despondent like that and says anything like, "There's no hope" be on high alert. There is a good chance that person has given up on life. I just recently lost a friend to depression and anxiety when she took her life last month. She was saying things like, "This is it. There's no hope." It didn't make sense. All who knew her loved her and her free, loving spirit. While she had overcome some adversity in her past, everyone thought she was doing fine.

If we recognize and admit our need for help, we can grow from the process.

She was an emotional person—both ways, but had always appeared to be living and loving life. Then a couple of difficult things happened to her and as her husband put it, "She seemed to lose her way and just couldn't find her way back." We all were shocked and saddened greatly by this as you can imagine. I share this because hopelessness really can trigger, especially someone clinically depressed, an emotion that takes them over the edge—so please be aware.

At times, most of us experience episodes of some form of depression, albeit it on a much lesser scale. Most of us experience discouragement, which might turn into the blues, causing us to get depressed and lose perspective. Remember, a certain degree of depression is normal. Even great spiritual leaders can get depressed. There are varying degrees of depression, so you are not immoral or sinful because you get depressed.

Grief over a tragedy or loss of a loved one is a type of depression. Anger turned inward is a huge reason so many people experience depression. If this is a problem for you, then you need to address and manage that misdirected emotion. If we feel someone has wronged us, we must learn the art of forgiveness, as I discussed in an earlier chapter.

If your depression lasts for a long time and moves into suicidal thoughts, losing your appetite, or being unable to get out of bed in the morning, you need to get medical help and see a counselor. Remember, there are three sources for your depression: physical, psychological (emotional), and spiritual causes. These are all intertwined and not separate entities. Our emotions are triggered by our thinking and perspective.

Usually, depression begins with wrong, warped thinking. That's why it's so important that as a Christ-follower, we must continually renew our mind by getting into God's Word and spending time in worship and prayer with Him. We need the truth in our lives. When we find ourselves slipping into that dark corner of depression, we need to remember God's faithfulness in our past. That can be colossal in getting our thinking back on the right track—when we focus on the goodness and faithfulness of God.

Unfortunately, how one reacts to their depression, anxieties, fears, etc. often promotes more of the same. Some are plagued a lot more than others, and some have learned to cope better than others, but there is relief for all of us if we know where to look for it. That is what I hope to accomplish through this chapter. I have learned the antidote to fear and uncertainty and want more than anything to share it with you because I believe you can find relief for your soul through the message I believe the Lord has given me to share with you.

What Is Anxiety?

According to Merriam-Webster, anxiety is "an apprehensive uneasiness or nervousness, an abnormal and overwhelming sense of apprehension and fear, possibly even mental distress or concern."[3] An anxious individual often anticipates misfortune, danger, or doom."

According to pastor Chip Ingram in a podcast he shared, the biblical word for anxiety means to take thought. It can be used positively, like taking thought of something positive, but usually, it refers to being obsessed with something that consumes the mind. It is often a fear of a future event, but sometimes it has to do with fear of something happening in the present. It could be anything and will be different for everyone. Another cause of anxiety is the form of regret for an issue that happened in the past.

> *Jesus promised us that we could absolutely have peace during difficult times.*

Here are some things anxiety can build up in us, spiritually, mentally, and emotionally. It can make us hyper-alert, irritable, fidgety, talkative, over-dependent; it can give us insomnia, poor memory, fainting episodes, excessive perspiration, muscle tension, headaches, including migraines, a quivering voice, hyperventilation, abdominal pain, nausea, diarrhea, and high blood pressure—to name a few. Wow. I want none of that!

Do you often wake up multiple times during the night and can't sleep, finding it difficult to get back to sleep? That's caused by anxiety. How do we change any or all of this? We do *not* have to live this way. Jesus promised us that we could absolutely have peace during difficult times. That is what I will try to unpack here in this chapter.

In John 14:27, Jesus tells us, "Peace I leave with you; my peace I give to you. Not as the world gives do I give to you. Let not your hearts be troubled, neither let them be afraid." Peter, one of Jesus's disciples, tells us in 1 Peter 5:7 to cast all our anxieties on God because He cares for us. Our God is a personal God who cares for us. He is all-wise, loving, and powerful and believe it or not, we are the object of His affection.

Paul, who wrote over half of the New Testament tells us in Philippians 4:6–7, "Do not be anxious about anything, but in everything by prayer and supplication with thanksgiving let your requests be made known to God. And the peace of God, which surpasses all understanding, will guard your hearts and your minds in Christ Jesus." When we become anxious about anything, we can run into His arms not only for comfort and compassion but also for guidance and direction in dealing with whatever our circumstance or need.

Through Paul, God is telling us to "Stop worrying." It eats up our soul. It ruins our emotions, thwarts our relationships, and can choke the life out of us. Worry does not empty tomorrow of its sorrow; it empties today of its strength. He will help you through this.

What does the second part of that verse tell us about how to get out of our misery? He tells us to pray with gratitude as we lay out our concerns to Him with the knowledge He will meet us where we are and will provide what we need. You notice it does not necessarily say we will get what we want. Sometimes that is not in our best interests. He knows better than we ever will, what we need to be who He created us to be. This is where we learn to put our faith and trust in Him. We need to learn how to pray believing. One thing we can count on is God never made a promise that was too good to be true.

When the red light on the dashboard of your car comes on, that is an indication something has gone wrong under the hood. When we lose our peace, that is a red flag—a reliable indicator that something is wrong with our focus and priorities. We are abiding in something other than Christ. The level of our internal peace serves as a monitor or barometer of our relationship to Christ.

What are You Afraid Of?

By nature, we like to be, or at least think we are in control of our life. When our life seems to be going out of control, we tend to comfort ourselves with things that give us a pseudo peace, don't we? It could be a box of chocolates or a bag of chips, a bottle of wine or pills, shopping for things we don't need, or maybe logging onto a website we should avoid. We have a propensity to be drawn to distractions that give us a temporary fulfillment and gratification.

Worry does not empty tomorrow of its sorrow; it empties today of its strength.

But then, the guilt pours in when we realize we have caved to our anxiety inappropriately in a way that has caused more harm than good. The whole thing can become cyclical if we aren't careful. When we do these things, we are not letting the peace of Christ rule in our hearts.

So what do we do when feeling anxious? When anxiety knocks at the door of our heart, let prayer answer it. God tells us that we are to take on an upward focus. It's pausing and remembering who God is and getting a high view of Him.

How do you think our loving God responds when we come to Him in prayer like that trusting Him to meet our needs? Imagine this. When a child is afraid of a storm causing loud, strange noises outside, what does he do? He runs to his parent's room and jumps in bed with them, right? What happens next? Within a couple of minutes, he is breathing heavily, indicating he is asleep, safe in his mother's or father's arms. That is how our heavenly Father wants us to rest in Him. Can you run into His arms and trust Him like an innocent child trusts his parents?

Living a life of anxiety is not a lifestyle that happens overnight, so we shouldn't expect to be free from it quickly. Life and its lessons are a journey, a marathon. God wants to help you with this, but He cannot steer a ship unless it is moving. You have to take those first steps of faith and surrender to a loving God who cares for you even more than a parent cares for their child. Then open your heart in prayer to Him.

Did you realize you can learn to be content no matter what your circumstances? The New Testament writer Paul came from an affluent background. He was well educated, a Pharisee, highly placed in the Jewish religion. He was a Roman citizen, so pretty much had it made by the world's standards.

> *The level of our internal peace serves as a monitor or barometer of our relationship to Christ.*

But then he met Jesus in a vision on the road to Damascus, where he was on his way to persecute the "Christ-followers" of his day. After that, he renounced all he had, took on a Christ-follower mission that resulted in his being homeless, beaten within an inch of his life several times, even left for dead once, shipwrecked, and imprisoned numerous times. Yet he said he had learned to be content whatever his circumstances because he served the living Christ, and that was all that mattered to him. Contentment is something we learn.

He tells us in Philippians 4:11–13, "Not that I am speaking of being in need, for I have learned in whatever situation I am to be content. I know how to be brought low, and I know how to abound. In any and every circumstance, I have learned the secret of facing plenty and hunger, abundance, and need. I can do all things through Him who strengthens me."

I have heard so many people say, "If this or that happens, then I'll be happy." It's all based on circumstances. Once they get the coveted achievement, then I so often hear something like, "That's it? Is that all

> *When anxiety knocks at the door of our heart, let prayer answer it.*

there is?" Jim Carey, the comedic celebrity, once said, "I think everybody should get rich and famous and do everything they ever dreamed of so they can see that it's not the answer."

I heard of a reporter who went to interview Muhammed Ali at his farmhouse, and Ali gave the reporter a tour. They ended up in his barn where all his trophies, ribbons, and memorabilia were showcased on the shelves gathering dust and even pigeon droppings. Ali softly said, "I had the world, I had *all* the world, and it was nothin'." So often I think we place too much importance on what other people think rather than what God thinks. Who really should matter in the long run?

I just quoted from Philippians, chapter 4, in which a few verses earlier, Paul tells us to be anxious for nothing, but with thanksgiving, we are to go to God in prayer with our needs. The book of Philippians is a letter he wrote to the congregation of a church he had started in Philippi, Greece. It has become known as "the epistle of joy" because Paul keeps referring to the joy of the Lord as his strength, giving him peace. Paul wrote this letter when he was in prison, so I would say he had mastered what it was like to rest in Jesus, Who gave him the peace and joy he could never have experienced without learning how to be content whatever his circumstances.

Contentment is not something to achieve; it is a secret to be discovered. We can learn so much from Paul. We need to learn that internal peace is not dependent on our circumstances. A couple of questions we occasionally need to ask ourselves are 1) what am I focusing on—what I do have vs. what I

> *We need to ask God what He wants us to learn, rather than telling Him what we want Him to change.*

don't, and 2) am I teachable? We need to remember a verse I shared early on: 1 Thessalonians 5:16–18, "Rejoice always, pray without ceasing, give thanks in all circumstances; for this is the will of God in Christ Jesus for you." We need to ask God what He wants us to learn, rather than telling Him what we want Him to change. Then we need to ask Him what needs to change in our lives so we can be more like Christ. If you did that, would that change your prayer life?

I know it seems like an oxymoron, but if we take the focus off ourselves and look with compassion as to how we can help others, that will bring us more contentment than the greed of always getting what we think we want and need. It is very counterintuitive, but you have heard it is in giving that we receive—and the measure with which we give is used to give back to us. So, if we give little, we will get little. If we give a lot, we receive a lot. Whatever we need, plant a seed. But be careful. Never give with the motive to get. Just give, and you *will* get in ways you never anticipated.

> *God's primary plan is not to make us happy, but to make us more like His Son.*

What Is God's Agenda for Us?

As I mentioned before, God's primary plan is not to make us happy, but to make us more like His Son. That really should be the goal of every Christ-follower—to be imitators of Him. How we respond to difficult circumstances gives us who follow Christ a platform to show how He makes a difference in our lives.

Who was Christ? Among many other things like saving us for eternity, we can point to Him as a role model in so many ways. We see He was full of grace and mercy, filled with humility as He exemplified the integrity of a servant leader, who led by example, showing compassion even to those who opposed Him. We can and should thank Him for our ups and downs because we know He has an overall positive plan for our lives. We learn on this journey that prosperity does not have the power to give us contentment; neither does poverty have the ability to take it away.

It is amazing how our life can change when we make gratitude for what we do have as our focus. It creates a heart change that can overcome just about any adversity. Only Christ can give us what we need to overcome our circumstances in life. Unbelievers tend to think that getting "things" will bring them contentment. The only problem is when the goal is achieved, as we have discovered, it doesn't deliver the expected gratification.

> *We learn on this journey that prosperity does not have the power to give us contentment; neither does poverty have the ability to take it away.*

It's very easy if we are not careful even as believers also to turn inward, chase a dream, thinking it's Jesus *plus* other things we desire that will bring us fulfillment. We can just as quickly get caught up in the lie that contentment comes from specific achievements or getting *stuff*. This is a pervasive lie that many of us get caught up in, and has contributed to a boom in Christian counseling because of the remorse and depression that follow our failure.

We must learn to believe the truth of the verse above from Philippians 4:13, "I can do all things through him who gives me strength" (NIV). That means Christ plus nothing. What would it look like if your circumstances had no power over your ability to be content and at peace? At the end of this great letter to the Philippian church, Paul is trying to encourage, and he says in 4:19, "And my God will supply every need of yours according to his riches in glory in Christ Jesus." I quote that knowing we sometimes get our wants and needs mixed up, but God doesn't, and He knows exactly what we need. The way we experience God's promises is to trust Him.

How Should We Deal With Fear and Anxiety?

How do we overcome this fear that wants to grip our hearts? If you are a Christ-follower, you will know the Bible tells us in many places that we are to "Fear not." We know Christ is with us, in fact, He is *in* us in the person of the Holy Spirit to give us peace during difficult and uncertain times. Jesus provides the answer for our fear. I don't mean to minimize all that is going on. We cannot control it for sure, but we can control how we respond to it. This mentality translates to anything negative that might be going on in our lives, not just this scary virus. It could be any negative situations that could easily take us down if we let them. Are we going to respond or to react? These are two very different things.

> *It is amazing how our life can change when we make gratitude for what we do have as our focus.*

We can choose to be grateful for what we do have and what's going on in our life that is good, or we can choose to focus on the negative and what we don't have. Life is full of choices. We can decide to make the best out of any situation in which we find ourselves, or decide to give in to fear and anxiety.

We have nothing to fear if we put our trust in the God who saved us. The psalmist David reminds us in Psalm 27:1, "The LORD is my light and my salvation, whom shall I fear? The LORD is the stronghold of my life; of whom shall I be afraid?"

God, through the prophet Isaiah in Isaiah 41:10, also tells us, "Do not fear, for I am with you; do not be dismayed, for I am your God. I will strengthen you and help you; I will uphold you with my righteous right hand" (NIV). What we focus on in uncertain times matters.

The way we experience God's promises is to trust Him.

Remember, in Matthew 14:28–31, when Peter went to walk on the water and took his eyes off Jesus and looked down at the waves? What happened when he took his focus off Christ? He started to drown, didn't he? Remember also in Mark 4:37–40 when Jesus was asleep in the boat, and the storm came up suddenly, and the disciples were afraid of capsizing? The only time Jesus ever really rebuked them was when they showed their unbelief and lack of faith in Him to take care of them.

Jesus expects us to trust Him when the wind and waves of misfortune confront us. If we let it, adversity can be a bridge that brings us to a deeper relationship with God. Fear, panic, and anxiety are emotions rooted in all the negative "what ifs" that *might* happen in the future. This could encompass any number of things, including financial loss, relationship crises, physical harm, or worry over any negative possibilities that *could* happen.

I want to share a portion of Scripture with you here. It's rather long but powerful. I love the whole section, and it will make sense when I share the following story with you. It's from Matthew 6:25–34)

> Therefore I tell you, do not be anxious about your life, what you will eat or what you will drink, nor about your body, what you will put on. Is not life more than food, and the body more than clothing? Look at the birds of the air: they neither sow nor reap nor gather into barns, and yet your heavenly Father feeds them. Are you not of

more value than they? And which of you by being anxious can add a single hour to his span of life? And why are you anxious about clothing? Consider the lilies of the field, how they grow: they neither toil nor spin, yet I tell you, even Solomon in all his glory was not arrayed like one of these. But if God so clothes the grass of the field, which today is alive and tomorrow is thrown into the oven, will he not much more clothe you, O you of little faith? Therefore do not be anxious, saying, "What shall we eat?" or "What shall we drink?" or "What shall we wear?" For the Gentiles seek after all these things, and your heavenly Father knows that you need them all. But seek first the kingdom of God and his righteousness, and all these things will be added to you. Therefore do not be anxious about tomorrow, for tomorrow will be anxious for itself. Sufficient for the day is its own trouble.

What I Learned about Fear

When my mom was diagnosed with Alzheimer's disease, I was fearful she might end up like my neighbor who had it for many years and turned into an extremely mean-spirited, high maintenance, nasty woman. My mom had always been so sweet, easygoing, and submissive. I knew if she turned out like this woman, it would be emotionally draining and challenging for my dad, who was her primary caregiver during her last years.

They had always had a close, loving relationship, and I dreaded for my dad to have to experience and put up with that type of behavior. I shared my fears with a friend I highly respected—about the same age as my mom. She urged me *not* to be fearful of what *might* happen because it may never happen. "Why worry about something that has not yet happened?" she told me, "as it may never happen, and then you will have worried yourself sick over nothing. If it does happen, then you will know it's not really your mom who is acting that way. It's the disease." She also gave me some

What we focus on in uncertain times matters.

Scriptures to encourage me in this area. She was right. My mom never acted out like my neighbor. I was glad I listened to my mature friend, and I always remembered that. Twenty-six years later, I still remembered that lesson when confronted with another opportunity to resort to fear, but based on what I learned from her and the Scriptures, I chose not to. I'll tell you that story in chapter 12.

There are always lessons we can learn in all our life experiences, especially the hard ones, if we are open to learning what they are. Besides that, based on God's promises in the Bible, we can be assured He will be with us, walking through the storms of life with us. He will never leave us or forsake us (Hebrews 13:5).

ARE YOU FEARFUL OF YOUR FUTURE?

When our focus is on all that could possibly go wrong in the things mentioned above, fear will most likely rear its ugly head. When Jesus was talking with His disciples in the upper room, just before He went to the Garden of Gethsemane to be arrested and taken to the cross, He told them some difficult things. He expressed that even though He was about to face death and they would face persecution or even death, that they need not be afraid. "Let not your hearts be troubled. Believe in God; believe also in me. In my Father's house are many rooms. If it were not so, would I have told you that I go to prepare a place for you?" (John 14:1–2).

He promised them they would live in a world of tribulation, difficulty, and persecution, but He told them, "I have said these things to you, that in me you may have peace. In the world you will have tribulation. But take heart; I have overcome the world" (John 16:33).

As a Christ-follower, you understand perfect love casts out fear. If you have experienced the saving grace and love of Jesus Christ, you know it is possible to experience peace when we encounter the storms of life. We are in a position to model calm and confidence in a loving, caring God, knowing He is sovereign, He's in control, and He has our back. He is faithful and unchanging, and having our best interest in mind, He will provide what we need when we need it. Faith in our faithful God allows us to live fearlessly and show how He equips us to live no matter what we might face during uncertain times. "In the same way, let your light shine before others, so that they may see your good works and give glory to your Father who is in heaven" (Mathew 5:16).

If we let it, adversity can be a bridge that brings us to a deeper relationship with God.

Peace comes from salvation—deliverance from our enemy—in our case, our sin. Romans 5:1 tells us, "Therefore, since we have been justified by faith, we have peace with God through our Lord Jesus Christ." You notice that is present tense "have" peace with God. This isn't just for when we die. It is for now *and* forever.

Diving Deeper

1. Do you or a loved one suffer from any form of fear, anxiety, or depression? Can you share the struggle?

2. How has that been dealt with in the past? What are some ways of escape that some of those afflicted use to distract themselves from their problem? Explain why or why not those ways are helpful.

3. After reading this chapter, do you see some different, more life-altering and sustaining approaches to combat these struggles? Please share.

4. What is your impression of how fear, anxiety, and depression are related, and what are the main underlying causes usually for any one of these?

5. What has been your experience or knowledge or opinion of the use of drugs to help any of these emotions? Has that changed at all after reading this?

6. What were some of Debby's recommendations as to what to do when overcome by any of these emotions? How can that be acted out, and how could you use what you have learned to help someone going through a difficult time?

7. What are some Scriptures Debby shared that could be helpful in dealing with these issues? Are you aware of some other scriptures that would also be appropriate and helpful to remember during difficult times?

8. What can we learn from Paul, who experienced incredible adversity since becoming a follower of Christ? How can we apply that to our lives?

9. From where does contentment come, and what is the possible role it can play in our lives?

10. This is a pretty heavy chapter. What are your major takeaways? Has it changed your outlook at all on these emotional responses to adversity? Do you think it will change your response at all the next time you experience a difficult situation?

Chapter 11

Life Lessons Learned From a Shepherd

Sometimes Jesus, our great Shepherd, needs to take us through a dark valley to get us where He needs us to be. If that happens, we can count on Him to walk closely with us, reassuring us of His presence, love, and compassion through it all, and we will come out the other side with an even stronger faith, more profound love, and closer relationship with Him.

Do you ever wonder, "Where is God" when going through challenging times? Does He seem distant, non-existent? We can be sure the one who has moved or shifted is not God. He is immutable (unchanging). What is the biggest crisis you are experiencing right now?

> *"Where is God" when going through challenging times?*

While you're thinking about that, I will attempt to unpack and explain a psalm that is so familiar that there is a tendency to gloss over it and think, "Oh, I know that psalm. I even memorized it as a child. It's usually read at funerals." Well, I bet there is so much more to this psalm than you ever imagined. At least that's what I discovered when the twenty-third psalm was explained to me by an actual shepherd, Phillip Keller, in his book, *A Shepherd Looks at the 23rd Psalm*.[1] Keller was a sheepherder for over a decade in the hills of Australia.

This will take a while, so why don't you grab a cup of your favorite beverage and get comfortable. I will take my time to explain why understanding this psalm may help you appreciate your Shepherd's heart and how He can help you get through your current valley or storm. There is so much to this, so like an onion, I will peel back one layer at a time.

Let's be clear that this was written as a metaphor. Camp out on this, so you don't miss anything. As you read my descriptions of the sheep and shepherd, to get the lessons from this message, please continuously think about the correlation between us as the sheep and God as the shepherd. See if you can find all the connections.

First, I will provide it below so you can review it to refresh your memory, or if you don't know it, you can follow along. As you read it, notice how personal and intimate it is with all the personal pronouns, "I," "me," and "my."

THE LORD IS MY SHEPHERD
A Psalm of David. (Psalm 23)

*The LORD is **my** shepherd; **I** shall not want.*
*He makes **me** lie down in green pastures.*
*He leads **me** beside still waters.*
*He restores **my** soul.*
*He leads **me** in paths of righteousness for his name's sake.*

*Even though **I** walk through the valley of the shadow of death,*
***I** will fear no evil, for you are with **me**;*
*your rod and your staff, they comfort **me**.*

*You prepare a table before **me** in the presence of my enemies;*
*you anoint **my** head with oil; **my** cup overflows.*
*Surely goodness and mercy shall follow **me** all the days of my life,*
*and **I** shall dwell in the house of the LORD forever.*

At the time David wrote this, readers understood the metaphor as they could relate because they understood sheep and the shepherd's role. In America, most of us are not very knowledgeable about sheep or shepherding, so we need a thorough explanation.

Many times throughout Scripture, we are referred to as sheep. It's not complimentary, but rather than be offended, let's see if we can learn why we are compared to them. First, let's understand a few things about sheep. They are slow, defenseless, and dumb, to put it bluntly. They are defenseless as they are afraid of their own shadow. Without help, they cannot find food or water and won't drink from a babbling brook because they are afraid of its noise. That's why a shepherd will often dam up an area of a stream, creating "still waters" where he can then guide the sheep to drink safely and without fear.

Rather than looking for greener, fresher grass, they'll eat grass down to the roots, ruining the pasture, and unless the shepherd guides or leads them to fresh grass, they'll die. If they happen to end up on their back, they cannot get up without help from the shepherd.

The shepherd was the lowliest job there was. It was always the youngest son's job to care for the sheep. They were to carry a "rod"

> *He may have to do some work in you before He can work through you, but as long as you are open to Him, He has promised to meet you.*

> *The Shepherd is not just a provider but the protector.*

in their belt, which was used to slay or scare off any predator trying to harm or take away their sheep. They also would carry the "staff," which was used to guide the wandering sheep back into the fold or lift it out of a bush or ravine where they had wandered off and gotten stuck. Occasionally, they might even give them a little rap on the behind to let them know they had gone astray and were not to do that.

Here's another great lesson. If a sheep continually wandered away, the shepherd, to protect the sheep from getting lost and, therefore, to die, would purposely break the sheep's leg, lovingly put it in a splint and then carry it around his neck so that they could bond, while the wound healed. When the bone had healed, the shepherd would put a little bell around that sheep's neck, and he would be called the bell sheep. He would stay close to the shepherd, and the other sheep would hear that bell and would follow.

There are many names for God, like Yahweh and Jehovah, but the Good Shepherd is also one of them. He is Eternal, Creator, the list goes on. You notice David starts this psalm, "The Lord is *My* Shepherd." The fact he referred to God as "my" Shepherd made it one of the most intimate, personal names we have for God. In his day, they understood a good shepherd protects, provides, and cares for his sheep. He understands, nourishes, and loves his sheep. It's a humble, lowly, serving job.

Here we have sheep described as very vulnerable, but they also are treasured. They provide sustenance (milk and lamb for food), and they can be sheared. Their wool can be sold to provide for other family needs.

Compared to the goodness of God, we are like sheep. When it comes to living life in light of eternity, we can be just as dumb as sheep.

We can be as vulnerable as they are, but to God, we also are valuable. The Good Shepherd is not a God who is way out there, shaking His finger when we mess up. He is a God who intimately cares about each one of us.

> *No matter what our darkness, we can count on His presence.*

If you look closely at the way this psalm reads, there are some statements about the present, but several about the future, which shows David's confidence in God's continued provision. We can learn how to be just as confident in God providing what we need, especially if we look at how He has done so in the past.

Now let's walk through this and see if we can learn what David understood about his Great Shepherd. He starts out saying he has no wants because his Shepherd will provide all his needs. We all have physical, psychological (emotional), and spiritual needs and are all intertwined. Here David tells us his Shepherd meets *all* his needs. He has *no* wants. He doesn't necessarily meet *your* wants or agenda, but He promises to meet your physical, psychological, and spiritual needs all the days of your life. He can do that only if you *let* Him be *your* Shepherd.

"He restores my soul." Restore here means to repent or even to be converted, giving grace. He puts back and holds together. He holds us up, much like with an invisible hand. Soul here refers to our psyche. As for spiritual issues, He guides and gives direction, putting us on the right path.

The other option is to think you are a pretty big sheep (feeling somewhat self-sufficient) with pretty good (reasonable, logical) ideas and the ability to handle things on your own—to graze where *you* think you will be fulfilled. You think you prefer your water and live life on your terms. What happens when a real sheep thinks that way? It's a disaster for him, isn't it? Our problem is that deep down, we are proud and arrogant. We want to be our own sheep and our own shepherd. Grace always follows humility, but humility is hard for human sheep to swallow—to admit our need.

This does not just apply to Old Testament times. I hope you see the connection here about a shepherd and our Shepherd. To come full circle—back to Paul in the New Testament, remember his exhortation in Philippians 4:19, "And my God will supply every need of yours according to his riches in glory in Christ Jesus."

What was true then is true now. Whatever your crisis, if you bring your life under the leadership and Lordship of the Shepherd, God promised He will be there to meet your needs. He may not meet them your way or on your timetable, but you can be sure it will be best for you in the long run. He may have to do some work in you before He can work through you, but as long as you are open to Him, He has promised to meet you.

When David says he is not afraid of evil, he means harm of any sort. How can he say that? Because he has confidence his Shepherd is *with* him and will protect him from *all* evil of any kind. So the Shepherd is not just a provider but the protector. He says, "Your rod and your staff, they comfort me." He is there to protect us from the enemy and others who might harm us or lead us astray. But sometimes, He might even have to protect us from ourselves.

Whether we want to acknowledge it or not, there is an invisible war going on through which the enemy wants desperately to tempt you to get your focus off God and onto yourself and your current difficult circumstances. He wants to fill your heart with fear, doubt, and overwhelming anxiety. His goal is to destroy you, and that can manifest itself in many different ways. You may find yourself getting angry and giving in where you are most vulnerable.

At the same time, however, if you are a Christ-follower, the Holy Spirit inside you wants to turn that same temptation into a trial He can use for your good as you learn to let Him be your provider and protector. When seen as a trial, you can see by faith that God has allowed it to provide an opportunity to persevere, thereby increasing your confidence as it was intended for your growth. By faith, you can choose to consider it all joy, and as you endure it, God's character is developed, and your life is transformed more into the image of Christ.

God tells us if we come, wherever we are, He'll meet us there and give us just enough grace for that moment.

If you should need a little shot in the arm concerning the benefits of trials, read the first chapter of James in the New Testament. Here is an excerpt from James 1:2–8:

> Count it all joy, my brothers, when you meet trials of various kinds, for you know that the testing of your faith produces steadfastness. And let steadfastness have its full effect, that you may be perfect and complete, lacking in nothing. If any of you lacks wisdom, let him ask God, who gives generously to all without reproach, and it will be given him. But let him ask in faith, with no doubting, for the one who doubts is like a wave of the sea that is driven and tossed by the wind. For that person must not suppose that he will receive anything from the Lord; he is a double-minded man, unstable in all his ways.

> Then James 1:12–15 says:

> Blessed is the man who remains steadfast under trial, for when he has stood the test he will receive the crown of life, which God has promised to those who love him. Let no one say when he is tempted, "I am being tempted by God," for God cannot be tempted with evil, and he himself tempts no one. But each person is tempted when he is lured and enticed by his own desire. Then desire when it has conceived gives birth to sin, and sin when it is fully grown brings forth death.

Don't give in, give up, or let go. This crisis you are going through now, or any dilemma you may have in the future, may make you more like Jesus than you have ever known, or it could pull you completely away from Him. The choice is yours.

We're not finished with this psalm yet. We are now at the part where David says, "Even though I walk through the valley of the shadow of death, I will fear no evil." Sometimes they have to take the sheep through terrain of ravines and valleys to where there is fresh, lush grass. When they have to walk through these ravines between two mountains, the shadows cause darkness, and that is where a shepherd will most likely lose some sheep.

Predators seem to know they can go there undetected. So this metaphor illustrates any darkness, any crisis, the darkest of times, or fear of the unknown. David reminds us that we don't need to be afraid because the Good Shepherd is with us. As they passed through that hazardous area, the shepherd would gather the sheep in close to protect them.

No matter what our darkness, we can count on His presence. Do you remember when Paul was suffering from some sort of physical affliction, and he asked God three times to remove it from him, but God said, "No?" Sometimes, when God has bigger plans than ours, He will say, "No." In Paul's case, He added, "My grace is sufficient for you." Paul then went on to say in the same verse (2 Corinthians 12:9), "Therefore I will boast all the more gladly of my weaknesses, so that the power of Christ may rest upon me."

God tells us if we come, wherever we are, He'll meet us there and give us just enough grace for that moment.

Remember, we said the rod was to fight off the enemy? Whenever you are in the dark times of your life, then that is when the enemy will swoop in and throw lies at you and cause you to experience all kinds of limiting beliefs. The wrong voices in your head will encourage you to take shortcuts that will take you down paths of destruction.

Our Shepherd has a rod to take down the enemy. In Ephesians 6:10–18, God, through Paul, tells us that we have armor and weaponry (in Him) to protect us with His power. As we go through a difficult time, we have to realize God has a game plan bigger than us to get us through it.

He may be pruning us. What happens when trees and bushes are pruned? New growth is stimulated, and they are reshaped to be more beautiful than if left alone, don't they? He may need to prune us, to change us, and you can be sure it will be for the better.

It's during the dark times that, if we seek God, we will find Him waiting with open arms to be what we need Him to be.

When life is running smoothly, we aren't exactly seeking God for counsel are we, especially compared to when we are down. We tend to forget God when things are running smoothly, don't we? It's during the dark times that, if we seek God, we will find Him waiting with open arms to be what we need Him to be. We do not have to be "in want" because our great Shepherd will meet all our needs. While we may experience some degree of fear, we are not to be paralyzed by it.

> *Inside, there is a life overflowing with that inner joy and peace that can only come from the Great Shepherd.*

At this point in the psalm, David changes the metaphor of his culture, celebrating who God is to a banquet and rejoicing. Banquets were lavish celebrations, often after a victorious battle—a demonstration of deliverance. Food and drink would flow freely while the defeated enemy would be forced to watch this celebration. It was a great time of fellowship and merriment.

Here he refers to the joy of experiencing the abundant, eternal life in the present, not just in the afterlife. This is relating to joy spilling over from the inside out—an assurance in an abundant life now and forever—a confident trust in the Great Shepherd regardless of circumstances, no matter how grim they may seem to be. Inside, there is a life overflowing with that inner joy and peace that can only come from the Great Shepherd.

In biblical times, battles between nations were over a conflict of deities. Pagans worshipped many gods, and this celebration was to honor the true God and show off their victory as proof their God was bigger and better than their gods.

There Can be no Christianity Without the Cross

What Cross are You Bearing Right Now?

I hope the explanation of this psalm has helped provide some comfort to you regarding that crisis I asked you about earlier that may be experiencing right now. I'd like to shift our mindset just a bit now to remind us that our "cross" is God's will for us, no matter what the cost. If you expect a relationship with God that does not require some suffering or inconvenience, then you can't use Christ as your example. God's will for you is to take up the cross He gives you. First, you must take up your cross, then you can follow Him.

Paul reminds us in Romans 5:3-5: "Not only that, but we rejoice in our sufferings, knowing that suffering produces endurance, and endurance produces character, and character produces hope, and hope does not put us to shame, because God's love has been poured into our hearts through the Holy Spirit who has been given to us."

We can live with confidence because our "hope" is in the faithful one, the Good Shepherd.

Our "hope" is not a "hope so" hope but a "know so" hope as we trust in God to be our guide, protector, and provider. We can live with confidence because our "hope" is in the faithful one, the Good Shepherd.

Diving Deeper

1. What do you think of the analogy of us to sheep and God to the Great Shepherd? Explain both and why it's such a good analogy.

2. Have you ever been in a situation where you felt like you were walking in the shadows, through a dark valley, wondered where God was and why He seemed silent? How did that make you feel, and what did you do about it? Do you think you would feel differently now?

3. What is something new you learned from this psalm?

4. Explain your takeaway regarding the rod and staff as it relates to God's protection, provision, and discipline.

5. Explain what you got out of the point of breaking the wandering sheep's leg, then nurturing it during the healing process.

6. What is the significance of the newly bonded sheep becoming the "bell sheep" the others listened to and followed?

7. Do you have a new appreciation for the intimacy between the shepherd and his sheep as it relates to us and our possible relationship with our Great Shepherd? Explain the examples given and the correlation to us.

8. What does this psalm say that can give us encouragement as to our Great Shepherd's provision and protection—providing whatever we need?

9. Did you pick up on the fact we are considered valuable? Explain how that makes you feel.

10. How can the lessons of this chapter, help you with your current trials? How has it changed your outlook on God's provision regarding perceived adversity?

Chapter 12

The Impact of Prayer

I have mentioned prayer several times in the previous chapters. Still, I want to take a little time to emphasize just how powerful and essential prayer is to experience a victorious Christian life. This is another topic on which many books have been written, but I wish to make a few critical points about prayer in a believer's life. To wait on God is our highest and most important work. The Holy Spirit comes to help us to engage in believing prayer.

I got a new appreciation for the power of prayer just last year after a particular "traumatic" incident in my life caused me to understand what it means to surrender. I have always believed in the power of prayer and pray daily in my quiet time and throughout the day when the Lord would bring someone to mind who needed prayer. It has become a way of life for me, but sometimes my prayers have not been full of life, meaning they were occasionally kind of rote, without the passion, care, and concern that should have accompanied them.

Then it happened. My husband fell off the top rung of an extension ladder when descending from our portico (the roof over our front porch), which he had been repairing. He flipped and landed on the top of his head on the edge or our flagstone step, falling about eighteen feet. I was standing right there, holding the ladder and watched my greatest nightmare happen before my eyes. In a split second, his body was lying on the ground next to me.

As I bent over him, I could see blood immediately pooling under his head. My heart lodged in my throat and about stopped as the moaning from his lips filled my tender ears. He never lost consciousness. I could see his head was split open all across the top and along the back. Blood was literally pouring out of it. While I'm kneeling over him in shock and trying to figure out what to do, a lawn service guy from across the street saw Bob on the ground with me bent over him and the ladder up against the roof. In what seemed like an eternity but was probably just a few seconds, he ran over and asked how he could help. I asked him to sit with Bob while I ran inside to get a roll of paper towels as he was bleeding profusely.

Bob was sitting up against this man and had blood all over him when I came back out. I rolled up a wad of towels and told Bob to hold them up to the top of his head where he was bleeding the most. I asked the gentleman to see if Bob could stand up and, if so, to help me get him in the car. We live less than two miles from a hospital.

What I thought I was dealing with was probably brain trauma and brain damage when I saw his skull split open like that. To be honest, I didn't even think about paralysis because he moved around on his own. He was sitting up and then got up and walked to the car!

In retrospect, I never should have moved him. But I was going on what I saw and figured I could get him to the ER quicker if I drove him. We live less than two miles from a hospital.

To wait on God is our highest and most important work.

When we got to the ER, they immediately did a CT scan and found out he had shattered his C1. That is called the atlas and is at the top of the spinal column and supports the base of the skull. It is ultimately what connects the head to the spinal column. There was more. If you are a medical person, here is the actual doctor report you might find interesting:

Spinal Fractures:

1. Comminuted (shattered) C1 ring fracture
2. Left occipital condyle comminuted (shattered) fracture
3. Right occipital condyle nondisplaced fracture
4. Left C6 lamina
5. Left C7 articular pillar
6. T2 compression fracture

We have shown this to numerous medical doctors, chiropractors, medical imaging specialists, etc., who have said no one walks away from this. One friend of ours, who is a medical doctor, told me when he first saw this report, he wept because he was sure Bob was paralyzed. When he heard Bob was released a day and a half after surgery, he said it was nothing short of a miracle. The physician's assistant said that they perform very few surgeries like his because usually, people don't survive a fall like that with his type of injury. My husband is a walking miracle.

Let's back up now. In the first ER, we had no idea yet the extent of the damage to his body, but all the medical staff who entered the room asked him to wiggle his fingers and toes and asked if he had any tingling or numbness. That's when we both realized they were concerned about paralysis. Unbeknownst to me, Bob had prayed, "Lord, however this turns out, let it be for Your glory." I weep even now as I write this thinking about how God answered that prayer.

When the CT results came back, they said they wondered how Bob even walked into the hospital. They advised he would have to be transported by ambulance to the trauma center at a different hospital, as they could not treat him there. That meant transferring him from gurney to gurney to gurney. Every time he was moved, there was a chance for something to go wrong.

I stood there thinking, "They seem so worried about paralysis, but I won't let fear overtake me about this because it hasn't happened yet, and it might not happen. If it does, we will deal with it, but right now, I won't be overcome by fear." Of course, I am praying under my breath the whole time that God would protect him. Remember the lesson I learned about fear regarding my mom and her Alzheimer's? I was able to carry that lesson over to this situation. God prepared me for this twenty-six years earlier.

I learned something exciting about this as time went on, and there was an opportunity to reflect. Bob observed and shared with me that God is not constrained by time (2 Peter 3:8). I had not even had time to ask anyone to pray yet because everything happened so fast.

As soon as possible, while in the first ER, I texted our three adult children to pray, just saying something to the effect of "Pray for Dad. Bad fall off ladder, in ER." Later as I drove to meet Bob and the trauma team at the other hospital across town, I called a friend to send an emergency email to an extensive list of our friends to ask for prayer. One thing led to another as word like this travels fast. Then my daughter put it up on social media, and in no time, there were well over five hundred people praying for us.

The thing is, when I was in the first ER, no one even knew to pray for me when I had such peace about the whole paralysis thing. Then, all along, I just had this assurance everything would be okay.

That same friend who sent out the email dropped everything and met me at the second ER. I think she was kind of concerned about me because typically, she knows I am a very emotional person, and yet I was not showing any emotion during the whole process. I just seemed to have supernatural strength. God knew all those prayers would be coming in on our behalf, and He answered them before they were even prayed. God gave me just the grace I needed when I needed it. He is always right on time!

While in the second ER, they unwrapped his head dressing, and blood squirted out. That was when we realized he had severed an artery. That's why there was so much blood. If I had not been there when it happened, he could have bled out right there on our sidewalk. He had been going up and down that ladder the previous weekend while I was out of town, and he was home by himself. Thank heavens I was with him this time.

We have never before been on the receiving end of so much prayer, and I can tell you, it is powerful. Against all the odds, Bob came home early from the hospital—only a day and a half after receiving a titanium plate screwed into the base of his skull and connected to two titanium rods screwed into his C2–C4 vertebrae. He had thirty-three staples in his neck after surgery, along with about eighty stitches in his head. He never was in ICU. No rehab as expected. He was able to remove the brace he wore home after four and a half weeks instead of six to twelve as predicted. No collar to follow the brace as expected. No brain damage or brain injury at all, and obviously, no paralysis.

I will never know if this is the case, but Bob's accident may have actually prevented him from having a worse one later on. We have a much higher roof to which he would climb on a more extended ladder to clean our gutters from leaves several times a year. A fall from that ladder would most probably result in death. Now I know at least that will not happen since he has vowed to me never to climb an extension ladder or to go on the roof again.

Yes, he is fused for life and has limited mobility in his neck, but we will take that any day over the alternative. Doctors are amazed he didn't die or at least become a quadriplegic. We feel so blessed and know it was because of the power of prayer. God obviously isn't done with Bob yet. He has had numerous opportunities already to tell his story and testify to God's provision and protection. He has surrendered in obedience to whatever God leads him to do. His answer is. "Yes, Lord, now what is it You want me to do?"

I have not for a moment, sensed an ounce of self-pity or "woe is me" from him about this. Sure, he has to live with a new normal that is far from ideal, and he has restricted movement. But here is another life fully surrendered to the Lord who he knows has given him an extra measure of grace and genuinely blessed by God. Despite this traumatic event, Bob's attitude of gratitude has enabled him to experience a victorious life. I know God has already used Bob to strengthen the faith of many who have seen his remarkable recovery and positive attitude.

I feel doubly blessed—that the outcome was so positive, and also that I don't have to live with the guilt of causing paralysis by moving him. I feel like there had to have been angels holding his head on as we went to the hospital until he could be stabilized with surgery. You know the song, "Angel Armies" by Chris Tomlin?[1] That song has taken on special meaning for me since my husband's accident. I shudder to think I could have caused the love of my life to be paralyzed. I believe God protected me from that despite my ignorance. I cannot tell you how grateful I am.

We look at this experience as a blessing not only because God spared Bob from a possibly much worse outcome, but also because of what we experienced firsthand about the power of prayer, of God's provision, and His protection. We learned how much our friends and community love us, and it made us realize how much we all love each other as a family. Our family is scattered all across the country, but all three of our adult children dropped everything and came immediately to be here for their dad and support me. Our focus has undoubtedly shifted to sharing more about God's goodness and how to experience a victorious life.

GENERAL THOUGHTS ON THE PURPOSE AND IMPORTANCE OF PRAYER

Just a few more general thoughts on prayer before we move on—ultimately, in prayer, we are to be seeking God's will in all things. What is prayer? It's actual death to self by saying, "God, we can't do this 'thing' without You." It's acknowledging we need Him. When we don't pray, it's like we're saying, "I *don't* need You and can do this on my own."

Our purpose in prayer is to connect with our Lord so He can transfer His will into our lives, enabling us to collaborate with Him to accomplish His goals and join Him in whatever He is doing. He uses our prayer time to soften our hearts and change our focus.

I have realized I sometimes have a hard time loving and even caring about some people I come across, and I have had to ask God to help me see and love others as He does. We cannot be intimately exposed to God's heart and remain complacent. The time spent with Him will transform our hearts and make us more like Christ.

Prayer is faith turned inside out.

If we want to be like Christ, we need to do what He modeled for us. What did He do? He made silence, solitude, and prayer a priority. Many times in Scripture, the writers tell us Jesus went away to pray. He pursued His Father. In quiet solitude, let the Holy Spirit create serenity in you.

If we continue to look to Christ for an example in prayer, look at the Lord's Prayer in Matthew and again in Mark, which He gave us as an example of *how* to pray. He started with praise (Our Father, in heaven, hallowed be your name). For our prayers to be powerful, we should always begin in praise. Why? First, because He deserves it, but also because praise is an expression of faith. It is not rooted in our circumstances, but in God's nature and trustworthiness. Prayer is faith turned inside out. When we pray in God's will through faith with clean hearts, we have every right to expect God to answer us.

He uses our prayer time to soften our hearts and change our focus.

For a Christ-follower, prayer is necessary and should be our first response, not our last resort. I love this quote from Corrie ten Boom, "Is prayer your steering wheel or your spare tire?"[2] Throughout Scripture, Jesus said, "when" you pray, not "if" you pray.

Whether we are praising Him, thanking Him, interceding for a friend, or petitioning for our own needs, we must be sure our prayers are God-centered and not self-centered. I was challenged just this summer by one of my pastors when he asked us if we were to see the answer to our prayers from the previous week, who would be the beneficiary, others or just ourselves? Would the world be a better place or just our little world? God wants to give us the desires of our heart, but our motives must be pure and right. He is a rewarder of those who earnestly seek Him. He longs to bless us like a father to a child.

Sincere prayers come from hearts that long to know God's will and desires for our lives. Our passion and purpose should be to bring Him glory. This often requires a quiet time of listening. Conversations need to be two ways. Sometimes, if you don't know how to pray in a particular situation, you need only ask the Holy Spirit help you pray because He certainly knows circumstances we don't. We need only express our concern and desire for God's will. "Likewise, the Spirit helps us in our weakness. For we do not know what to pray for as we ought, but the Spirit himself intercedes for us with groanings too deep for words" (Romans 8:26).

He is a rewarder of those who earnestly seek Him

Whenever I pray for myself or others, I tell God what my/our desire would be for an outcome, but that ultimately we want His will because we know even though it may be difficult to accept, we know His ways are best and for a purpose. I have to admit that was a difficult prayer in this situation when my husband's life, as well as my future, were at stake. That is a lot easier to say as a mantra, than when it is so personal, but I did it, and I know God does not always answer our prayers as we hope, but so thankful He did this time!

To say the time we invest in prayer is time well spent is an understatement. There is no better way we can spend our time. That is why Paul, in the Bible, tells us to "pray without ceasing" (1 Thessalonians 5:17). It is for our benefit.

For a Christ-follower, prayer is necessary and should be our first response, not our last resort.

God is deeply touched by our struggles and loves it when we come to Him, asking for help. Often He is just waiting for our invitation to step in to provide whatever it is we need. Sometimes we just need to surrender a problem into His hands and ask Him to take control. James reminds us in 4:2-3, "You do not have, because you do not ask. You ask and do not receive, because you ask wrongly, to spend it on your passions."

> *Our view of God will shape how we pray, and prayer is an integral part of our relationship with Him.*

Our view of God will shape how we pray, and prayer is an integral part of our relationship with Him. When we pray, our motive should not be to have God respond in a specific way to our requests as much as to express our trust in our loving Father who cares so much for us and knows better than we, what we need. When you pray, do you come to God with absolute confidence He will answer?

What are some roadblocks that can keep us from experiencing answers to our prayers?

1. We don't ask or ask with the wrong motives
2. Known, unrepentant sin
3. An unforgiving spirit
4. Improper treatment of our spouse or others—disunity
5. Lack of generosity—selfish ambition
6. Lack of faith

Any of these can be considered a "kink in the hose" or a "blood clot" that blocks our communication from God.

Can I confess something here? When I need God's help or intervention, I am quick to pray and eager for His response and hearing from Him. However, sometimes, I am almost afraid to ask God to speak to me. Why? Because I know when He speaks, I must either do what He asks or face disobedience if I don't comply. Do you ever have that problem? We need to remember, anything He impresses upon us to say or do will be for our good and His glory, and it is our responsibility to be obedient.

A couple more things to keep in mind when we pray for someone is we need to prepare to be a part of the solution for which we are praying. We cannot just shoot up a prayer and hope God or someone else He assigns to help will cover the need without our willingness to become involved in the solution. Another thing is we need to be sure while it is important to pray in faith, our faith mustn't be in our prayers but in the God to whom we pray.

> *Our faith mustn't be in our prayers but in the God to whom we pray.*

As I experienced during my husband's accident, the Lord can provide a transcendent peace and tranquility that is incomprehensible in the place of worry. When asked how we could have so much peace during such storms, we can honestly say we have no idea. We know our hope is in the Lord; He is good, He is sovereign, He is in control, and we can trust Him. Nothing else can bring such comfort.

Our primary goal in talking with God through prayer is to seek intimacy with Him. If we seek Him first, we will have everything we could ever need, even those things we didn't realize we needed. Matthew 6:33 says, "But seek first the kingdom of God and his righteousness, and all these things will be added to you."

> *If we seek Him first, we will have everything we could ever need, even those things we didn't realize we needed.*

Diving Deeper

1. What is the purpose of prayer?

2. What are some examples of answered prayer you have experienced?

3. Before reading this chapter, had you ever thought about God answering prayers before they were prayed? Looking back on your life, can you see when that may have happened?

4. Have you ever personally experienced or know of a situation where multitudes were praying for someone, and you saw a miraculous recovery? Tell about it. How did that affect your faith?

5. What can we learn from situations where God doesn't always answer our prayers as we hoped He would?

6. Explain a time when you or someone you know thought God didn't answer a prayer, but later found out the "unanswered" prayer was actually answered in a way far better.

7. What can we learn from Christ about His prayer life?

8. After reading this chapter, has your mindset shifted regarding the importance of prayer? In what way and what changes do you plan to make regarding your prayer life?

9. What are some important things to keep in mind as you pray?

10. How does God look at prayer? What does He want from us, and how do you think you could most please Him with your prayer life?

11. What are some roadblocks that could keep you personally from experiencing answers to your prayers? In other words, what do you struggle with that could be a hindrance to your prayers getting answered?

12. Are you sometimes a bit afraid to pray because you fear God will ask you to do something you don't want to do? If your answer is yes, rethink how much you want to experience the intimacy and fulfillment of God in your life. Talk about that.

Chapter 13

Practical Application for Experiencing the Life You Always Wanted

I will include a methodology in this section to provide some helpful disciplines that can assist you to experience a victorious life daily. These are just suggestions that have worked for me. You may already be doing these or even have others that work better for you.

You have incredible potential to do great things for God. Just remember the Christian life begins and ends with "grace." You were saved by grace, and it is that same grace you are to extend to others in your sphere of influence as you share what God has done for you.

If you ever feel like you are failing or not measuring up, know that God will not love you any more or less than He does right now, and nothing you do or don't do will change that. Since you have read this far, I know you have a desire to be a man or woman of God. What follows are suggestions about how to experience a daily intimacy with your risen Creator, Savior, and Lord. May you have confidence in the Holy Spirit's power that lives in you, to be an instrument, a life preserver to a dying world.

We need to look to Christ as our ultimate example and servant role model.

First, how can we surrender ourselves to the Lord? It's a matter of yielding our body, mind, will, and rights to God. How do we do that?

> *The Christian life begins and ends with "grace."*

Through disciplined prayer. It's only when we yield to God's will that His power can then take over and give us the *"will"* power, and the *"won't"* power to be a victorious Christian. We need to look to Christ as our ultimate example and servant role model. Below are some daily disciplines I have found helpful.

DAILY DISCIPLINES TO EXPERIENCE THE VICTORIOUS LIFE

- **Upon Waking:** Try developing an attitude of gratitude before even getting out of bed. Think of several things for which you are thankful.

It has been scientifically determined it is physiologically (and therefore emotionally) impossible for the brain to experience gratefulness and dissatisfaction at the same time. So, we have to choose what we will place our focus on.

We often don't have control over what happens to us in our daily life, but we do have control over how we respond. If we have started our day with an attitude of gratitude, we are more likely to respond in a godly way.

According to neuroscientists in studies at the University of California and the University of Miami in 2015, maintaining an attitude of gratitude affects one's outlook on life. It contributes to more positivity, improves sleep quality, reduces anxiety and depression, as well as reduces the risk of heart failure, among other findings. It also has been found to release dopamine, which is a pleasure hormone.[1] I certainly see no "downside" to developing a lifestyle of gratitude!

Practical Application

- **Before Rising:** Ask the Holy Spirit to help direct your day, so you don't waste time doing insignificant things.

Time cannot be redeemed. Once it's gone, it's gone. We can always find ways to make more money, but we can never manufacture time. That's why giving your time is such a gift. We need to make sure we are using it wisely and for His good.

- **Pray:** Ask God to show you sin in your life that you need to confess, and ask Him to show you what it looks like to totally surrender to Him. Then just sit quietly and listen. Then follow through with confession.

- **When you get dressed:** Ask God to clothe you with the love and humility of Christ. Then ask the Holy Spirit to remind you as a believer, you were given the mind and heart of Christ and to notify your face, so you have the countenance of Christ. ☺

This is so you can be an extension of Him to everyone you come into contact with that day.

- **Look in the mirror - What do you see?** We want others to see Jesus in us, so we have a platform to share Christ—no matter what our environment.

We were created to be a visible example of Christ's invisible character. This includes all of the fruit of the Spirit, which embodies His character: love, joy, peace, patience, kindness, goodness, faithfulness, gentleness, and self-control.

- **Morning Quiet Time:** Take time first thing in the morning before you start your day to have a "quiet time" of prayer and Bible Study. I have a Christian music playlist on my phone, and I play that as I shower and get dressed in the morning. In the Appendix in the back of this book, I have a list of some "Attributes of God" along with a short definition of each and a Scripture to accompany each one. What a great way to start your prayer time—focusing on a couple of different ones each day with which to praise Him.

> *Praise and adoration will put you in a positive frame of mind.*

Praise and adoration will put you in a positive frame of mind. Pray for others, then pray for enlightenment as you spend some time in the Word. Even if you only have time to read a few verses and a short devotional, at least do that. If at all possible, try to make time to do more. It'll be worth it, and you'll be glad you did.

Devotionals are great to highlight the meaning of Scripture and to provide the application of it, but it's the Word of God itself that transforms us. It contains the Truth that sets us free.

We mustn't forsake the reading of Scripture to just listening to sermons or reading devotional books. While those are all good things and serve a great purpose, they should be in addition to reading, studying, and meditating on Scripture. It's the Word of God that leads us to the heart of God. As a Christ-follower, we are to live and die by this Book, so we need to know what it says. As we study the Scriptures, we gain a deeper understanding of who God is. We see His character, understand His heart, and learn His promises.

If we want to be like Christ (which should be our goal as a Christ-follower), we must study Him to know Him and His attributes. We learn that through Bible Study. Besides coming to save us from our sins, God also sent Jesus to be a model, a revelation, a representation of how He wants us to live our lives. We are to emulate His character.

> *It's the Word of God that leads us to the heart of God.*

Just like we spend our disposable income on what is important to us, we also spend our time the same way. If experiencing

Practical Application

the victorious life is crucial to you, you will want to invest the time in God's Word.

If you make it a point to do these things every day for a month or so, they will become a way of life, and if you haven't been doing these things, I think you will find a real change in yourself which will probably spill over/rub off onto others around you. There—you have changed your legacy and increased your intimacy with Jesus.

Be sure to become part of a small group and challenge one another in the faith. It's so important to be in fellowship with other believers. As I mentioned earlier, we cannot live out our faith in isolation and who we hang out with is important.

We cannot live out our faith in isolation and who we hang out with is important.

PRACTICAL APPLICATION

DIVING DEEPER

1. What is one of the best ways Debby talked about to demonstrate you are surrendered to the Lord?

2. Do you already have some daily disciplines that help you to connect with God to get you through the day? If so, what are they?

3. Debby gave us a list of six things she does and recommends. Which of these resonates the most with you that you have not been doing but want to add to your daily routine?

4. Before reading this, did you know your brain could not be grateful and dissatisfied at the same time? How will that affect your choices throughout the day now? If you knew that, can you share how your experience bears that out?

5. As you self-reflect, realizing you cannot redeem time, what are some ways to make better use of your time, to be sure you are doing all you can for the glory of God? What do you need to give up?

6. Are you living intentionally to be an extension of Christ to those who need to see what that looks like? How—in what way?

7. How have you been challenged to improve or start your quiet time with God to get His guidance and direction for your day? What changes do you plan to make?

8. If you don't already have one, what kind of Bible reading strategy do you plan to implement to make sure you are in the Word every day to learn the heart or God?

9. Did you realize before this just how important confession is to keep clear communication open between you and the Lord? How will you be more intentional about that from now on?

10. If you are not already in a small group, will you seek one out and become an active member?

Chapter 14

Best Practices Going Forward
Next Steps
to Take Your Life to the Next Level

Now that you know all you do about how to experience a victorious life, what will you do with that knowledge? At the end of our life, everyone—even Christ-followers will have to give an account of what we have done with our lives and all the gifts and blessings which we have enjoyed while here on earth while awaiting our heavenly home. Will your life be a tribute to the matchless grace God has given you? What is one thing you need to say "No" to? What is one thing you need to say "Yes" to? Are you ready to "pay it forward?" Are you going to live a life worthy of the calling (Ephesians 4:1)?

We are all products of our past, but that does not have to define our future. If you have been dealt a lousy hand by poor upbringing and dysfunctional role models, with God's help, you can break those bondage chains. You must, because, especially if you are a parent, you should not expect your children to end up any better off than what they have been taught and saw modeled in your home. We parents have a huge responsibility to exemplify Christ to our children. We might be able to fool others outside the home that "all is okay," but our children know us like no one else and will see hypocrisy in a heartbeat.

> *We are all products of our past, but that does not have to define our future.*

The heroes of the faith were all ordinary people like you and me with no personal power. Their ability to excel was the mighty presence of God in their lives. Times change, but the effect of God's presence remains the same. In at least 99.9 percent of the testimonies we have heard in the marriage enrichment program my husband and I facilitate, the couples sharing indicated the turning point in their marriages was when they both individually got serious about their relationship with the Lord. As a Christ-follower, you have the *same* power!

> *Remember, you are God's masterpiece, created in His image, conceived in grace and love.*

Remember, you are God's masterpiece, created in His image, conceived in grace and love. If you allow Him to, He will mold your life in a way that glorifies Him. "For we are his workmanship, created in Christ Jesus for good works, which God prepared beforehand, that we should walk in them" (Ephesians 2:10).

You can walk in victory because Jesus is your example, and His Spirit lives inside of you. As you approach the finish line of your life, do you have an eternal perspective?

Please don't be like those in the half-empty lifeboats floating in the Atlantic when the Titanic went down. Many passengers were saved, sitting in half-filled lifeboats, but were afraid of returning to those who were floating in the frigid water needing to be saved. Those in the lifeboats could have saved some in the water, but they hoarded what they had, which, if they had shared, could have saved many lives.

Every life matters to God. Just before Jesus ascended to the Father, He told the disciples:

> *You can walk in victory because Jesus is your example, and His Spirit lives inside of you.*

"All authority in heaven and on earth has been given to me. Go therefore and make disciples of all nations, baptizing them in the name of the Father and of the Son and of the Holy Spirit, teaching them to observe all that I have commanded you. And behold, I am with you always, to the end of the age" (Matthew 28:18-20).

Like the rest of the Scriptures, that command (not a suggestion) was not only for the disciples but also for all of us. The culmination of the victorious life is to share what you have learned with others so they can learn to experience the fullness of God for themselves. There is nothing more rewarding than joining the Holy Spirit at work, bringing others into God's family. Sometimes all you have to do is share what Jesus has done for you. A lot of tools are available that show how to share your faith (See my resource list in the back of this book).

How can we let those we know who are lost slip away into eternal destruction when we know the way to eternal life? The most significant thing you can do is to invest in them, to help them into your lifeboat before they slip away forever. If you genuinely believe all you have just read, how can you keep silent? I know you are afraid of being rejected. Yes, you might experience rejection. We all struggle with that to some extent. However, we should be playing our life out to an audience of only one—God. No one else's opinion should matter.

I know that's a lot easier said than done unless you have the gift of evangelism, but God calls all of us to take a step of faith to share what we know about Jesus. Once you have led that first person to Christ, you will

> *Your ability to influence the world is directly proportional to your relationship with Jesus.*

be so emotionally charged and blessed by God, you will be looking for the next opportunity! The emotional and spiritual reward is incomparable to anything else on this side of eternity.

It is a fact when people are on their deathbed, thinking over their life, they never regret what they *did* so much as what they *didn't* do, the risks they did *not* take, their complacency regarding important, meaningful things and relationships. God never promises us tomorrow, so we should not procrastinate, putting off until a later time what we can do for God's glory today.

> *You have a unique DNA, skills, talents, and gifts that God has purposed for you to use for His glory.*

Remember, there are sins of "omission" (those things we *did not do* that the Holy Spirit prompted us to do) as well as sins of "commission" (the sins we *do* commit). Sometimes sins of omission are the result of an attitude of maybe we will comply when we have more time, or it's more convenient. Perhaps we haven't done *bad* things, but we have been disobedient in *not* doing the *good* things. Ouch!

You know what? You will probably find a lot of people are surprisingly open and are not opinionated at all about the gospel. They may genuinely be curious and interested, especially if they have been going through a rough time, and you might appear to be offering hope. Maybe just ask their permission to share what Christ has done for you.

It's essential to be genuine and winsome when sharing your faith, so they know you are sincere, genuinely care about them, and don't think you feel superior. Just realize if you stay inwardly focused, you could miss the opportunity to lead these unbelieving co-workers, neighbors, family, and friends to eternity in heaven.

Living in America, we tend to believe everyone has at least heard of Jesus, and there are plenty of other Christians go around sharing their faith. Not so. One of my pastors shared just this week he was at a restaurant waiting for his food and engaged in conversation with a woman from Viet Nam who has been in this country for twenty years, living in Loudoun County, Virginia.

They were talking about her heritage, her faith views, and so on. Then he asked her,

"Hey, have you ever heard of Jesus Christ?"

"Who?" she responded.

He said, "Jesus Christ, the Son of God, the message of the Bible."

She said, "What? I don't know what you are talking about."

Pretty unbelievable, isn't it? That bothers me a lot. I hope it bothers you as well. We don't have to go overseas as a missionary to spread the good news of the gospel. We probably don't even have to leave our neighborhood. One cannot accept or reject what they haven't even heard.

You have no idea how God can and will use what He calls you to do. We just need to be obedient and do it.

Many in this current generation are growing up in homes where God and Jesus are only mentioned as profanity. Spiritual things are not the topic of their conversation, and these individuals are growing up having no concept of the importance of having a relationship with the living God.

When the Lord opens the door for you to share your faith with someone, then that means He has been pursuing that person. He also is preparing their heart to hear and possibly even receive your message.

> *The greatest joy you will ever experience is when God uses you to bring joy to others.*

Not only that, but He will also give you the words to say. If you are surrendered to Him, you just need to shoot up a quick prayer, and He will provide the words you need to say. This experience might be a "crisis of belief" moment for you as you trust Him to speak through you. Then, when you talk, you will know it was of God.

Remember, you are just a messenger—an instrument to speak the truth. It is the Holy Spirit's job to convict and to lead an individual to saving faith. Maybe you are just called to plant a seed, or perhaps to water one someone before you planted. You may even have the opportunity to reap the harvest, but if not, you have at least done your part by being obedient.

The Bible gives us "life or death" information, and it is our responsibility and privilege to share it. You were put here on this planet for a reason, one of which is to be in an intimate relationship with your Creator, spend eternity with Him, and bring as many people with you as possible. Your ability to influence the world is directly proportional to your relationship with Jesus. Your mission is to know Christ and to make Him known.

Consider the magnitude of that calling. We are not called to a religion or duty but to a relationship—with the living God where we are seen as holy and blameless in His sight—not because of anything we did, but because of what Jesus did for us on the cross.

> *Your legacy can be established by no one else on earth.*

We are called to a purpose. There is no one like you. You have a unique DNA, skills, talents, and gifts that God has purposed for you to use for

His glory. He has a purpose only you can fulfill because there is no one else like you. We are to do good works that He has prepared and planned for us even before we were born.

Following Jesus will lead you into experiences you never thought possible.

We have a general purpose to love God and people. We have a specific purpose which, when we discover it, becomes our holy ambition. When you discover your unique purpose and you begin to give your life away, carrying out your specific call, He will use you to make a difference even if it is just what you think is a little corner of your world. You have no idea how God can and will use what He calls you to do. We just need to be obedient and do it. When that happens, the spirit of God causes you to experience the peace of God and there is nothing like it. The greatest joy you will ever experience is when God uses you to bring joy to others.

Your personality, calling, and gifts are unique, and God has devised a blueprint with your name on it, specifically for you. Your legacy can be established by no one else on earth. Your strengths, struggles, and situations are not hit-or-miss but divinely appointed for God's work.

We need to be careful not just to get busy doing "good" things. No amount of activity, even for God, can ever take the place of a heart that is right with Him. Remember the most important commandment? We are to love the Lord our God with all our heart, soul, mind, and strength, then our neighbor as ourselves. Love God and the person in front of you. What is success in God's eyes? Obedience and loving others with the unconditional love we have received from Him.

There is no denying; we will leave a legacy when we die. The question is, what kind will it be?

Following Jesus will lead you into experiences you never thought possible. You will find yourself feeling Jesus's pain as you see those trapped in sin as well as His joy in seeing lives redeemed. You will see broken lives made whole, the spiritually blind to see the truth for the first time. You will see marriages and individual lives restored, those in bondage and addictions released.

I mentioned before I am an emotional person. If I see someone else in tears, I'm right there with them. I don't even need to know what the problem is. My heart is touched by any suffering I see, whether it be physical or emotional. I am even quicker to tear up when I see or hear a touching story of redemption, answered prayer, etc. For many years, I was upset that I was so emotional. I used to ask God why He made me that way because it was often embarrassing.

My kids knew when to look over at me in a situation when I would have tears in my eyes, and they would always be right. Then one day, God reminded me I had the mind and heart of Christ, and I had asked Him to break my heart for what broke His. So, I would feel His pain, but also I would rejoice when He would rejoice—like over a lost soul redeemed. I still tear up whenever I hear a testimony of a transformed life or see evidence of His intervention like He showed in my husband's accident. When I realized God had just given me a tender heart like His, I was okay with the way He made me. I now consider it a God-given gift. If you feel like your life experiences have hardened your heart, you can ask for the Holy Spirit to soften your heart as well.

There is one thing that cannot be taken from us when we die, and that is our influence.

There is no denying; we will leave a legacy when we die. The question is, what kind will it be? What we should hope people remember from being in relationship with us, is a Christ-like life. They should remember the joy of Jesus demonstrated with grace and humility. They should be inspired to live a life of self-sacrifice and service that exemplifies Christ because of our example. There is one thing that cannot be taken from us when we die, and that is our influence. It will live on and hopefully with a positive impact. Some of our heroes in the faith are even more powerful today than when they were living.

We may be the only Bible our friends and family will ever read and the best Christian they will ever know. We are to be a "living epistle." It is so important to "walk the talk." It's easier to talk about the victorious life than living it, so our lives must demonstrate Christ-like behavior. We don't want people to remember *us* so much as what we represented—Jesus. Everything should point to Him. We are merely ordinary people serving an extraordinary God. We also should be living as if today was our last because someday it will be. Remember, we are not guaranteed tomorrow. Every day we live puts us closer to death, and our diagnosis is terminal. Our son and daughter-in-law have a plaque in their house that reads, "Every day is a gift. That's why they call it the present."

We are merely ordinary people serving an extraordinary God.

Your obedience now will provide a legacy of faithfulness to the next generation. While on the topic of legacy, do you realize when you faithfully, continually pray for someone, your prayers may outlive you and come to fruition years later? Never stop praying. You may pass away, but the impact of your prayers will not.

Remember my friend who was facing an early death by cancer, and what an inspiration she has been to me? I want to follow her example and finish well. Who has been an inspiration to you? (By the way, on a side note, during the few months it took me to write this book, my friend transitioned into the arms of Jesus when the chemotherapy destroyed

> *Your obedience now will provide a legacy of faithfulness to the next generation.*

her kidneys, and she went into renal failure. I'm so glad she knew Jesus! Her passing is a reminder to me of just how short life can be, and we never know when anyone's last day on this earth might come.) We need to be so diligent in sharing the love of Christ to anyone who does not yet know Him.

Whether you realize it or not, your life and how you present yourself has the potential to bless everyone you encounter. Some things to think about: Are others strengthened and encouraged in their faith because of their relationship with you? Do you usually look at others merely with the thought of what they can do for you, or are you striving to be a positive influence, looking for ways to help, encourage, and inspire them?

Has God given you a vision of what you can do to help further His kingdom? He will undoubtedly champion and support any idea He provides, but we won't see it unless we give that vision legs and step out in faith to pursue it. We must take action for God to use us. He cannot steer a ship unless it's moving.

Whatever you do, don't let Satan deceive you into thinking because you may not do any *great* thing (in your opinion), you cannot do anything at all. I am always inspired by stories by famous, well-known Christian leaders who share how some unknown person introduced them to Christ. If those individuals had not followed through with the promptings of the Holy Spirit to share their faith, these prominent Christian leaders would not have the fantastic, eternal influence they have today. You just might be the one to usher into the kingdom some such individual. Remember,

> *Your life and how you present yourself has the potential to bless everyone you encounter.*

you are to "let your light shine before others, so that they may see your good works and give glory to your Father, who is in heaven" (Matthew 5:16).

Let me close with a somber example of what we certainly don't want to be our legacy. You don't want to be a stumbling block for anyone—especially someone not yet in the faith. For the last sixteen years, my husband and I have been mentoring married couples in our church who have raised their hands that they are struggling in their marriages.

> *Peace comes in knowing God's grace is sufficient and will sustain us even in our most difficult circumstances.*

For the last six years, we have also facilitated small groups with a biblically-based marriage enrichment curriculum. Not everyone who attends is from our church or any church for that matter, as it is advertised online, and we never know who might respond, and we are happy to work with anyone who wants to improve their marriage.

This story comes not from one of our groups, but from a group led by a couple who are friends of ours. They told us every couple in that group had some significant issues they are trying to overcome. One of the program's ground rules is no one is to throw their spouse "under the bus." They are to work on themselves and their relationship with God and pray for their spouse without blame-shifting. The couples are allowed to bring up concerns they are working on in their marriage, but only if done respectfully.

Well, things had been heated apparently for several sessions, and there had been arguing between spouses with a lot of finger-pointing. Here is the kicker: One man stood up and said,

"Look, I already know I'm going to hell, but you all call yourselves Christians and look at you. You can't even get along!"

First, how sad this man has no idea about the seriousness of going to hell. In his honesty, he almost was claiming that as a badge of honor. What he saw in the others were pure hypocrisy and a terrible witness. In his authenticity, he called it out for what it was. To give this group a little credit, at least they were there because they knew their marriages were in trouble, and they needed help. The problem is, they were sure their spouses were the problem, not because they had no relevant relationship with Christ, who, through the Holy Spirit's power, is the only one who can give them the help they need.

Quite honestly, I wanted to write this book because I have witnessed so many individuals unhappy in their marriages, and I know—I can see the evidence they are not surrendering their lives to God. They may or may not read the Bible, but so many are *not* being obedient to what they *do* know. If we want to grow in the truth of what the Bible teaches, that is inseparably connected to the truth you already know. What do we call that? Obedience. Only obedience satisfies God's desire for obedience.

The Word of God is not just a source of helpful suggestions. It is life itself! To study and obey it is the best way to experience all God has in store for us. Many say they love God, but they cannot get along with their spouse. There is a disconnect—something is terribly wrong there. Life is full of choices, and we must live with the consequences of those choices. If you base your life choices on the Word of God, time will be your defender, and the wisdom of your choices will be validated.

The "crucified life" is the "victorious life."

Many Christians, as I see it are stuck or living defeated lives, and I hope the contents of this book will help *you* understand while it might seem like an oxymoron, the "crucified life" is the "victorious life." When we "let go" of trying to control our life and "let God" be Lord, we can rest in Him and trust Him in His sovereignty and faithfulness to meet our deepest needs and provide whatever is necessary to get us through any circumstance.

> *He never calls us to do something without faithfully enabling us to do it.*

If you feel like you are wandering around in the wilderness, Jesus offers us a land of promise. He is our hope and our provider. He has already conquered the enemy. We have the shield of faith with which to deflect the fiery arrows of the enemy. He is our source of peace, joy, and power. By faith, we just have to trust His promises, die to self, and enter His rest. Peace comes in knowing God's grace is sufficient and will sustain us even in our most difficult circumstances.

As a Christ-follower, we have been given the mind and heart of Christ, which should result in the countenance of Christ, which enables us to be an extension of Him to everyone we meet. With His help, we can live a life of service, putting others' needs before our own, clothed with Christ's humility while living out the fruit of the Spirit. If you are unsure of your mission, ask the Holy Spirit what He would have you do. Realize also we go nowhere by accident.

Everywhere we go, there is a need. When we fully surrender to Him, He fills our hearts with His presence, takes complete control, and wins all our victories. He never calls us to do something without faithfully enabling us to do it. He is everything we need to experience the victorious Christian life. Hopefully, that defines the life you always wanted. What is your goal and plan going forward? How are you planning on investing the rest of your life?

If you know what God wants you to do, determine to accomplish it. Beware of distractions and other opportunities that might get in the way and cause you to lose sight of that goal. Don't succumb to the temptation to delay or even discard your obedience like I did when it came down to writing this book. Don't procrastinate as I did. To experience the victorious life, once you receive an assignment from God, with authenticity and full surrender, let your response be unwavering obedience—immediately.

> *Your ability to serve God is not based on your past but your faithfulness today.*

How do you know when you are successful in life as a Christ-follower? "By this all people will know that you are my disciples, if you have love for one another" (John 13:35). Forgiveness, prayer, knowledge of good and evil, reliance on God, suffering with one another, and compassion for others are how you know.

Your ability to serve God is not based on your past but your faithfulness today. Do you sense your life is part of God's timeless purposes? You bet it is! You are a significant part of something much bigger than yourself. As I have said time and again, blessings come as a result of obedience.

God desires to take you one step of obedience ahead of where you currently are to teach you to trust Him to the degree you never have before. Are you prepared for Christ to reveal Himself to you in ways that will change your life? Are you ready to step out of your comfort zone?

You have all you need to live an abundant, victorious Christian life of surrender. My prayer for you is when it is time to enter into your eternal home, you hear, "Well done, good and faithful servant."

Final Reflection:

What is our goal as a Christ-follower? We are to live our life for Him, to Him, through Him, with Him, about Him—everything in our life needs to point to Him.

DIVING DEEPER

1. Now that you know all you do about how to experience a victorious life, what will you do with that knowledge?

2. Going forward, what do you need to say "No" to? What do you need to say "Yes" to?

3. As you approach the finish line of your life, do you have an eternal perspective? Have you gained the confidence to carry your life out in a manner worthy of the calling for which you have been called? In what way?

4. Has God given you a vision of what you can do to help further His kingdom? What will you do about those things now to give them legs?

5. What limiting beliefs have kept you from moving on what you feel God has been calling you to do?

6. Have you thought that much about the fact we all have influence, and we all leave a legacy? What changes do you plan to implement in your life that will draw others to Christ and to put your life on a better trajectory of hearing, "Well done, good and faithful servant?"

7. Did you ever think about how your prayers live on long after you are gone? For whom do you need to invest more prayer time?

8. Has your definition of "Living the Life You Always Wanted" changed since you picked up this book? Has it taken you a different direction than you expected? If so, is that a good or bad thing?

9. In what way have you been challenged beyond your comfort zone? What will you do with that?

10. Which chapter of this book had the most impact on you and has stimulated you to make the most significant change in the way you live your life?

Epilogue

You already know all you need to share your faith with others. Just tell your story and what you know. Personal examples of redemption have the most influential impact. God won't do anything remarkable through you until He does something significant *in* you. Since you have stuck with this book to the end, I hope that means you have desired and experienced a new depth in your love for Christ with a passion for passing along what you have learned.

Remember, as you relate and share with others, it was a radical love that marked the early church and was so effective. We cannot give away what we don't have; however, you have Christ's love inside you. Remember, we must be winsome and authentic to the core, speaking the truth in love. Someone threw you a lifeline at some point in your life. Now it's your turn.

I started in the introduction with a couple of verse segments to challenge us as we walked through these pages. Now I would like to leave you with another exhortation from Paul found in Ephesians 4:1–3 as a take-a-way: "I therefore, a prisoner for the Lord, urge you to walk in a manner worthy of the calling to which you have been called, with all humility and gentleness, with patience, bearing with one another in love, eager to maintain the unity of the Spirit in the bond of peace."

If you would like additional resources on how to share your faith, or to back your claim that the Bible is the reliable Word of God, evidence Jesus rose from the dead, and various other issues skeptics might bring up as stumbling block for them, you will find a list of resources in the following pages that could help you.

It is not comprehensive, but among those is a book I wrote out of my concern for those who do not know what the Bible teaches about eternal life. They don't know what they don't know. In layman's terms (that's the only way I could do this), I briefly address these difficult to understand issues. I titled it, *Forever Is a Long Time to be Wrong.* I wrote it for the atheist, agnostic, and apathetic. It's a rather quick read for the skeptic or "none" (those who resist any religious label)—short and to the point—to help answer some critical questions about our faith.

Have you found this book to help you take the next steps forward in your spiritual journey? Have you identified areas where you have lacked obedience and need to surrender? If you think this book could help others, would you mind taking a few moments to leave a review on Amazon to let others know some of your takeaways? We all rely so heavily on those, don't we—especially if we are unfamiliar with the author. It would be a way to support this ministry for free and would mean so much.

I have prayed as I wrote this that every reader would come to understand how the "Crucified Life" is actually the "Victorious Life." I pray the truths I shared in this book have given you the tools to live the life you always wanted—one that experiences all the fullness of God. I pray you have experienced the perfect love of Christ in a new way as well as victory at some level, along with the peace, joy, and power of a surrendered life.

Be sure to check out my website: http://www.DebbySibert.com to get the latest information about all and my newest publications. There you also will find a contact form if you have any questions or concerns. In the "Author" section, you can see the topics on which I am available to speak for women's groups at your church or para-church organization. If you follow DebbySibertAuthor on Facebook, you will receive my daily inspirational quotes.

God Bless you on your journey,
Debby Sibert

Follow and connect with me on your favorite social media platform:

https://DebbySibert.com

https://twitter.com/debbysibert

https://www.linkedin.com/in/debsibert/

https://www.pinterest.com/debbysibert/

https://www.instagram.com/debbysibert/

https://www.facebook.com/pg/DebbySibertAuthor

Do You Want Debby's *Free* Follow-Up Book?

Debby always has a booklet available to help her readers along in their spiritual journey. These giveaways complement each of her books. The companion booklet for this book, a forty-page pdf, is a perfect follow-up from this book. It is titled, *Thriving in the Vine.* It's a study of "What it's like to live as a branch connected to the Vine of Life" discussed briefly in this book.

If you'd like to receive this free eBook and to be notified when she's launching any new free or paid books, please consider signing up at the following link. In fact, those who sign up will be the first to be notified when new books are available for purchase as well.

Whenever she launces a book, it is highly discounted at launch.

Check out this free booklet and download it for free here: https://tinyurl.com/ThrivingVine

Or use this QR code to access it.

Appendix
Attributes of God

This list is not exhaustive but contains plenty of God's attributes to blow the human mind about God's unfathomable character. I could quote dozens of verses to back up each attribute of God listed here, but I picked one for each to help if you would like to expand your knowledge and understanding of each.

Accessible – He lives in every believer, and we can access Him at any time. (Galatians 2:20)

Compassionate – The outpouring of Christ's blood to make grace available to all of us reflects God's compassionate heart. (Psalm 103:13)

Creator – No one Created God. There never was a time when He did not exist. Only He can bring something out of nothing, and He created everything. The same God who created the entire universe and all its galaxies created, loves, and knows you by name! He created us all for a special purpose. (Genesis 1)

Eternal – He always was and always will be. He exists outside the boundary of space and time. Because He is eternal, He offers us eternal life with Him, which He alone can give. (Romans 1:20)

Faithful – We can always trust Him in all things and to keep His promises. This is the basis of our confidence in Him. He can never *not* be faithful as that is part of His divine nature and would require Him to change. He cannot cease to be who He is. (Deuteronomy 7:9)

Father – He is Father only to those who believe in His Son, Jesus Christ. We are all His creation, but we are only His children if we are willing to call Him Father. He lovingly protects, cares for, and disciplines His children. He longs for an intimate relationship with us. (John 14:23)

Forgiving – Forgiveness is an outpouring of God's love. None deserve it, yet God offers it freely to all who accept the substitutionary, sacrificial death of Jesus Christ on the cross. (1 John 1:9)

Glorious – God's glory exhibits the total of all His many attributes. He is infinitely beautiful and magnificent, full of grace and mercy. The Lord Jesus reveals God's glory completely. His radiance and beauty emanate from all that He is and does. Our whole existence and purpose are to glorify and bring glory to Him. (Psalm 19:1)

Good – He is infinitely, unchangingly kind and full of hope and goodwill. We see God's goodness in His love and faithfulness. Even when bad things happen, God always promises to make all things work together for good. (Romans 8:28)

Gracious – Grace is God's kindness and favor to all of us who do not deserve it. He is slow to anger and great in lovingkindness. Grace is so much a part of God and so inextinguishable that He can no more hide it than the sun can hide its brightness. (Ephesians 2:8–9)

Guide – God is our light, illuming our path, guiding us in the way we should go. Without His direction, we would stumble and fall like those probing their way in the darkness. (Proverbs 3:5–6)

Healer – God is the great Physician and has the power to heal at will, miraculously, or through traditional methods. (Psalm 103:1–3)

Holy – God is high and lifted up and set apart above His creation. He is always perfect with a purity that is incapable of being anything other than what it is. Holy is the way God is, and He is the standard. He has set us apart to be holy as He is holy. Because He is holy, all His attributes are holy. (Isaiah 6:3)

Appendix

Immutable – God and nothing about Him will ever change. He cannot change. While it is impossible for man *not* to change, it is impossible for God *to* change. He will never be more or less holy than He is right now. Because He never changes, we can always trust Him and His promises. (Hebrews 13:8)

Impartial – It does not matter your status, race, or reputation. God saves people, regardless of what they have done or will do. God will always do right by every person in every situation. (Romans 2:11)

Incomprehensible – We will never be able to understand God's thoughts and ways, which are much higher than ours. Because of His Word and His indwelling Spirit, we can understand all we need to know. (Isaiah 55:8–9)

Infinite – God is self-existing, without origin. He is Eternal with no beginning and no end. He always existed and always will. God's love and power have no limits. God, the Father, Son, and Spirit are all the same: infinite. (Revelation 22:13)

Invisible – Since God is a spirit, we cannot see Him. However, God has made Himself visible through the person of Jesus Christ. We can experience Jesus's presence through the Holy Spirit with us now, and when He returns, we will see Him as He is, face to face. (Colossians 1:15)

Jealous – God's jealousy is far different than human jealousy. His is one of protective love. He is righteously angry when His children choose to devote their time and attention to lesser things. Out of His love for us, when we turn our back on Him, He pursues us with all that He has. (Exodus 34:14)

Joy – Just like God is love and truth, He also is joy. Our joy is rooted in who God is. We can experience internal joy no matter what our circumstances because God reigns. (Nehemiah 8:10)

Just – God's justice is unchangeably right and perfect. His decisions are always a reflection of His righteous character. Because He is holy, He cannot ignore sin. But, because He is just, God will never punish His children, who have put their trust in Him, accepting the sacrifice Jesus paid on the cross for our sins. (1 Corinthians 6:11)

Love – God has always been love. It's who He is. It is an essential attribute of God. If He stopped *loving*, He would have to stop *being*. His love never fails. The love of God is eternal, sovereign, unchanging, and infinite. God loves the world, and when we receive His Son as our Savior, then we have the capacity to love God and others with that save love. (1 John 4:16)

Merciful – Miraculously, God in His mercy does not give us what our sins deserve. He is unchangeably compassionate and kind. He forgives and restores those who humbly repent and turn to Him in believing faith. His mercies are new every morning. (Ephesians 2:4–5)

Omnipotent (all-powerful) – God has unlimited power, authority, and influence overall. He does all that He wills to do with no limits. Nothing can stop God or stand in the way of Him accomplishing His will. (Jeremiah 32:17)

Omnipresent (everywhere) – God is everywhere. There's nowhere in the universe where God is not present. There is no way to hide from God. Satan has restrictions and can only be in one place at a time, but God has the power to always be everywhere at all times. (Psalm 139)

Omniscient (all-knowing) – Nothing ever surprises God. He knows all there is to know. He possesses perfect knowledge and has no need to learn. He knows all our thoughts, words, and deeds. Only God knows all things, and we can trust Him to judge perfectly. (Psalm 147:5)

Appendix

Patient – God is patient – an attribute we would do well to learn. He could put an end to human rebellion immediately, but He loves His creation and does not wish for anyone to perish, so He allows time for repentance. He is slow to anger, but one day God will come to judge all people. (2 Peter 3:9)

Perfect – God is perfect and upright in everything He does and says. All His attributes, His revelation, His works, and His Judgments, are entirely free of fault or defect of any kind. Everything He is, does, or says is flawless and true, including His Word—the Scriptures. (Psalm 18:30)

Person – God is an actual person, not an idea or an impersonal force. We were made in His image, so like us, He has identity and personality. He is one being in three Persons, God, Son, and Holy Spirit, equal in essence, but each with their own function. All work together to accomplish our salvation. (John 5:26)

Preserver – When we become a Christ-follower, we can be assured that He will complete the work He began in us. There is nothing we can do to lose our salvation. He preserves us so that He can accomplish His will and purpose for us. (Philippians 1:6)

Provider – God provides whatever we need. He provides for our daily needs, as well as a way out of temptation, and protects us from evil. He is the great I AM, meaning He is ALL we could ever need. God's greatest gift to us is His Son. Because of that, we can trust Him to give us everything else we need. (1 Corinthians 10:13)

Righteous – We can count on God to be right in all He does. All His words, actions, and plans are always pure and right. God Has no sin, is perfect in every way, and certainly never lies. We can count on Him to be fair, just, and faithful in all He does. Because God is righteous, He expects us to be righteous as well. Even the best person cannot be perfectly righteous, but God sees His children through the blood of

Christ that was shed for us and therefore clothed with the righteousness of Christ. (Isaiah 41:10)

Savior – Thankfully, God reaches down and rescue sinners from the penalty of death and hell that we deserve. Because we are dead in our sin, we have no power to save ourselves. God's plan from the beginning was to save His children from the penalty, power, and presence of sin. He sent Jesus to live the perfect life we could not live, and He died in our place for our sin, exchanging His life for ours. On the cross, Jesus paid the ransom for us, which satisfied God's wrath against our sin. That leaves no punishment for us, His children. Jesus saved His children from sin's power and gives us new desires and a unique ability to fight sin through the power of the Holy Spirit, which indwells the heart of every believer at conversion. (2 Corinthians 5:21)

Self-sufficient – God has no needs. Because of this, we can go to Him to satisfy all our needs. He can do immeasurably more than all we ask or imagine according to His power at work in us. (Romans 11:33–36)

Sovereign – God controls all things, at all times, and there's nothing outside of His control. What God plans happens. Nothing happens out of His authority, and not even Satan can stop or change God's plans. He is free to do whatever He wants. When God permits evil, we can trust that in His faithfulness and sovereignty, He has planned to use it for our good and for His glory. No one can keep God from accomplishing His plan because He alone has the power to do it. (Luke 1:37)

Transcendent – God is exalted far above the created universe, so far above, that human thought cannot even imagine it. We should be in total awe of Him. (Psalm 97:9)

Wise – God is not only all-knowing. But also He is full of perfect, unchanging wisdom. He always uses His knowledge to do exactly what is right. The idea that God is infinitely wise is at the root of all truth.

Appendix

God's Word is full of His wisdom. All wisdom comes from God. As a Christ-follower, we have access to the wisdom of God. How amazing is that! If we are to be truly wise, we must seek Him. (James 3:17)

Resources
Recommended Reading:

For help In Sharing Your Faith:

Case for Christ, Case for Faith, Case for Easter, Etc. – Lee Strobel

Evidence that Demands a Verdict – Josh McDowell

Forever is a Long Time to be Wrong – Debby Sibert

Where Will You Spend Eternity? Not Sure? There's Still Time – Debby Sibert

For Help in Growing Your Faith:

Absolute Surrender – Andrew Murray

Breaking Free – Beth Moore

Experiencing God – Henry Blackaby

Follow Me - David Platt

Radical - David Platt

Radically Obedient, Radically Blessed – Lysa TerKeurst

Rewire Your Heart – David Bowden

So You Want to be Like Christ? – Charles Swindoll

Something Needs to Change – David Platt

What Every Christian Ought to Know – Adrian Rogers

What Happens When Women Say Yes to God - Lisa TerKeurst

My Favorite Devotionals

Experiencing God Day by Day – Henry Blackaby

My Utmost for His Highest – Oswald Chambers

Notes

Introduction:

1. Randy Alcorn. "Can You Know You're Going to Heaven?" Eternal Perspective Ministries, March 5, 2010. https://www.epm.org/resources/2010/Mar/5/can-you-know-youre-going-heaven
2. "Self-Described Christians Dominate America but Wrestle with Four Aspects of Spiritual Depth." Barna. September 13, 2011. https://www.barna.com/research/self-described-christians-dominate-america-but-wrestle-with-four-aspects-of-spiritual-depth/

Chapter 1:

1. D. L. Moody, *The Overcoming Life and Other Sermons.* (Chicago: Bible Institute Colportage Association, 1896) 15–16.

Chapter 4:

1. "G266 - hamartia – Strong's Greek Lexicon (ESV)." Blue Letter Bible. Accessed 18 Aug, 2020. https://www.blueletterbible.org//lang/lexicon/lexicon.cfm?Strongs=G266&t=ESV
2. Helen H. Lemmel, *Turn Your Eyes Upon Jesus.* Brentwood Benson Music © 1950
3. https://www.blueletterbible.org/
4. Brother Lawrence, *The Practice of the Presence of God.* (Grand Rapids: Spire Books, 1958) 44

Chapter 5:

1. Andrew Murray, *Absolute Surrender.* (Bloomington: Bethany House, 2003) Chapter 14
2. Ibid.

Chapter 6:

1. Andy Stanley, *Louder Than Words.* (New York: WaterBrook, Multnomah, 2004) 152
2. National Sexual Violence Resource Center (NSVRC); Statistics, https://www.nsvrc.org/node/4737 Accessed 20 Aug. 2020

Chapter 7:

1. Henry Blackaby, *Experiencing God.* (Nashville: Broadman & Holman, 1994) 212
2. "G5401 - phobos – Strong's Greek Lexicon (ESV)." Blue Letter Bible. Accessed 20 Aug, 2020. https://www.blueletterbible.org//lang/lexicon/lexicon.cfm?Strongs=G5401&t=ESV
3. D. L. Moody, *The Overcoming Life and Other Sermons.* (Chicago: Bible Institute Colportage Association, 1896) Chapter 7.
4. Ibid.

Chapter 9:

1. Rick Warren, *God's Power to Change Your Life.* (Grand Rapids: Zondervan, 1990) 42.

2. Corrie Ten Boom. The Hiding Place. (Bantam Books: 1982) 118

3. Mary Stevenson, Footprints in the Sand, 1936, https://www.onlythebible.com/Poems/Footprints-in-the-Sand-Poem.html

4. Hillary Scott, "Thy Will Be Done." https://www.youtube.com/watch?v=iCR_Fa8YV2U

Chapter 10:

1. "Fear." https://www.merriam-webster.com/dictionary/fear

2. "Depression." https://www.merriam-webster.com/dictionary/depression

3. "Anxiety." https://www.merriam-webster.com/dictionary/anxiety

Chapter 11:

1. Phillip Keller, *A Shepherd Looks at the 23rd Psalm* (Grand Rapids: Zondervan, 1970)

Chapter 12:

1. Chris Tomlin, "Angel Armies." https://www.youtube.com/watch?v=qOkImV2cJDg

2. Corrie ten Boom. *Clippings from My Notebook*. (T. Nelson 1982) p. 64

Chapter 13:

3. Masterpiece Living, Neuroscience Reveals: Gratitude Literally Rewires Your Brain to be Happier, 12-23-2019, https://www.countable.us/articles/38777-neuroscience-reveals-gratitude-literally-rewires-brain-happier

Other Books by Debby Sibert

God's Antidote
For Depression, Anxiety or Fear

Learn How to Experience Peace and Joy During Adversity and Uncertain Times

Do you ever wonder, "Where is God" when going through challenging times? Does He seem distant, or even non-existent? *What is the biggest crisis you are experiencing right now?*

We are currently living in extraordinary times, causing much anxiety even for the strongest temperament. There are many reasons individuals experience fear, anxiety, and even depression, and our world seems to be growing more and more fearful every day. If we ever lived in an uncertain time with an unclear future and reason to fear it is now.

Fear is a natural response for humans and has its place to help keep us safe. However, living in fear is counter-productive and is not an option if we are going to get through any difficult circumstances. We cannot allow ourselves to get stuck there and dwell on these negative issues.

Believe it or not, there is a way to experience peace in the midst of all of this and that is what I will be unpacking in this book. We have many choices in life. Every day we're making more choices than we realize. Peace is another choice that we can make over fear and anxiety. It takes recognizing where our mind is going and living with the intention to make a U-turn and choosing peace.

In this book, we take a hard look at fear, anxiety, and depression—defining them, discussing the symptoms and causes of each, and how to overcome them. One cannot read this book without being changed from the inside out if the shared truths are taken seriously, acted upon, and allowed to permeate and become a reality in the reader's heart and mind.

Unfortunately, not knowing how to respond often causes one to react to their depression, anxieties, fears, etc. in ways that promote more of the same. Some are plagued a lot more than others, and some have learned to cope better than others, but there is relief for all of us if we know where to look for it. That is what I hope to accomplish through this short book.

I have learned the antidote to the fear and uncertainty that often leads to anxiety and depression. I want more than anything to share it with you because I am confident you can find relief for your souls through the message I believe the Lord has given me to share with you.

WHERE WILL YOU SPEND ETERNITY
Not Sure? There's Still Time

If you do not yet know Christ and the reason you *must* have a relationship with Him, then you need to read my first book, *Where Will You Spend Eternity?* If you are not sure whether or not you're going to heaven when you die, this book is for you.

We live in a busy world, don't we? Do you find yourself living just in the present? Do you ever think much about or plan for the future—not just retirement, but beyond the grave?

What is your destiny? What will happen to you when you die? Do you know for certain where you're headed, or are you not quite sure? Do you even know how serious that question is? The Bible tells us that once we die, our body decays, but our spirit lives on forever. If that's true, and it is, then it's essential to know where you will spend eternity.

That's what this book is all about. You can positively know you will go to heaven, but not everyone gets to go there. The alternative destination is catastrophic, which you must avoid at all costs. It's essential to get that straightened out now while you're still alive and have the chance to change the trajectory of your life. If you let them, the truths in this book can truly change your life for eternity.

If you are a Christ-follower, you can join many others who have found this to be a great ministry tool in sharing the gospel with those you love, care about, and want to see in heaven! This is a short, quick read, and when taken to heart, it will change lives!

COMING SOON:

FOREVER IS A LONG TIME TO BE WRONG
What Is Your Destiny?

This book, *Forever Is a Long Time to Be Wrong*, is for those who struggle to believe there is a God or the Bible is true and relevant. In simple layman's terms, I help answer some hard questions, backed by thought-provoking evidence which I hope will challenge previous "preconceived" ideas about God, Creation, the resurrection, and the reliability of the Bible among other things.

Do you call yourself an atheist, agnostic, or a skeptic when it comes to God, Christianity, the reliability of the Bible, the validity of the resurrection, creation, and all those Christian buzz words? Maybe you're a "none"—someone who doesn't want to be associated with any religious belief.

Could it be that perhaps you have bought into a lie that all the above is false? Could it be you have accepted your parents' beliefs without doing your due diligence to research the truth for yourself?

Could it be you made a religious decision when you are a child based on what you knew at the time and are stuck there not giving it much thought now that you are older and more mature?

One thing we both can agree on is someday we will die. I'm telling you there are only two destinations—heaven and hell, and we don't just return to dust.

If you don't believe that, forever is a long time to be wrong. Once you leave this world, there is no chance to change your mind. It will be too late. The time to get that figured out and straightened out is now while you are still alive.

If you did not want to have anything to do with God while on this earth, He will not force you to spend eternity with Him. He will say, "*thy will be done,*" and you will be separated from Him or anything good *forever.*

The purpose of this book is to help walk you through some difficult questions with reliable evidence that hopefully will convince you of the need to make a U-turn. We are not promised tomorrow, and every breath we take is a gift. Please don't put this off!

God's Toolbox for a Fulfilling Marriage
Learn What the Required Tools Are and How to Acquire Them

For couples, this book, *God's Toolbox for Marriage,* is still in my head and my heart. I will get it in print as soon as I am able. My husband and I have been mentoring struggling married couples officially for over sixteen years, unofficially for decades. This is my passion because I know an amazing marriage is fully possible and am so sad that many couples never get to experience it, at least after the honeymoon period is over and reality sets in.

Any marriage help book is basically a toolbox of tips regarding how to get along with your spouse in the interest of having a successful marriage. Success looks different to different people, but it goes without saying and would be fair to conclude that we all want to be happy and fulfilled in our relationships.

In this particular marriage manual, before the various tools for communication, conflict resolution, etc., are discussed, the content is focused on the foundational principles found in Scripture which teaches how to live lives of obedience and surrender to Christ which then gives us the ability to love and serve one another as Christ modeled.

There is no way we can have the ultimate marriage without having the guidance and direction of the Holy Spirit to empower us to love perfectly with the integrity and humility of Christ. It *IS* possible, and this book will give you the tools, encouragement, and instruction to achieve an amazing marriage that is the envy of all who know you.

Made in the USA
Columbia, SC
19 June 2025